You Are What You Think

You Are What You Think

by Doug Hooper

PRENTICE-HALL, INC., Englewood Cliffs, N.J.

You Are What You Think
by Doug Hooper
Copyright © 1980 by Doug Hooper

Printed in the United States of America

Prentice-Hall International, Inc., London
Prentice-Hall of Australia, Pty. Ltd., Sydney
Prentice-Hall of Canada, Ltd., Toronto
Prentice-Hall of India Private Ltd., New Delhi
Prentice-Hall of Japan, Inc., Tokyo
Prentice-Hall of Southeast Asia Pte. Ltd., Singapore
Whitehall Books Limited, Wellington, New Zealand

10 9 8

Library of Congress Cataloging in Publication Data

Hooper, Doug.
        You are what you think.

        1. Success. 2. Self-perception.   I. Title.
BF637.S8H612   1981   158'.1   81-7377
                                          AACR2

ISBN 0-13-972984-4
ISBN 0-13-972976-3 {PBK.}

This book is dedicated to the many hundreds who have written telling me their lives have been changed by the teachings it contains. I know it will do the same for you, because it is based on teachings that have been handed down to us throughout the centuries. These teachings, which are based on Natural Law, are 100 percent infallible when put into practice.

Preface

The basic premise behind everything I have written is that anyone, no matter what his or her present circumstances, has the inner power to change his life for the better. One's happiness need not be dependent upon what others say or the manner in which they act.

It is *your* thoughts and *your* actions that are the determining factors in your life. It wasn't until I realized this that my world began to change. I saw that simply by changing my attitude toward myself and my environment the outer circumstances of my life could be controlled.

As you progress through this book I think you will find that you are not powerless to change your circumstances, and that no situation is unalterable.

There is a great spiritual force within each of us, but it is lying dormant until called upon and used.

There is a whole new world awaiting you.

Start now to discover it!

Contents

You Are What You Think

1

Daydreaming Can Be Worthwhile

Day dreaming is usually frowned upon, and one who does so is often thought of as being lazy and lacking ambition. I don't agree. Day dreaming can be very constructive.

Isaac Newton was once asked how he discovered the Law of Gravity. "By thinking about it," he answered.

There is a vast difference between day dreaming and mere wishful thinking. Wishful thinking is vaguely hoping for circumstances to change, although you don't really expect them to do so.

Day dreaming is visualizing something you would like to have or a state of being you wish to achieve.

"You become what you think about most of the time," said Emerson. Constantly holding the attention on that which you want tends to attract it to you.

This does not happen by chance. Of course, it works for your detriment as well as your betterment. The end result is dependent upon your choice of thoughts.

Unfortunately, day dreaming has fallen into disfavor because many overlook the fact that it is necessary to act as well as to dream. However, if one remains open to the

3

possibility of changes in his life, it will become natural to act in the manner best suited to him.

As one grows older, hope for changes for the better to take place may diminish. Day dreaming becomes more centered on the past than on the future, more of the "might-have-beens" rather than what might be. This is tragic.

Someone wrote long ago, "There is not much to do but bury a man when the last of his dreams is dead."

Some experience this feeling of futility and others never experience it. Age is not necessarily a factor. For example, the person who is lonely and without friends must understand that it is within his power to change the situation.

The first step one must take is to start thinking of himself as being a friendly person. Use of the imagination can create great changes in one's life.

He should think of himself as being surrounded by friendly people even while alone. This abrupt change in one's thoughts actually causes a change of consciousness.

When a person changes inwardly — which begins with a change in his thinking — his outer circumstances must change. He will soon find himself becoming involved in activities entirely different than anything he has engaged in previously.

If one's opinion of himself is low, it must be raised. This can be done by thinking about his good points to the exclusion of those he considers bad.

Don't be afraid to day dream of a happier future. When one ceases to dream, it is usually an indication he has lost hope.

At this point, a gradual withdrawal from life takes place, perhaps unconsciously, and the chance for any more than a dreary existence is lost.

It is unfortunate that we were not indoctrinated at an early age with the knowledge of the importance of our thoughts.

The lonely, depressed person looks around him and says: "But it is true that I don't have any friends, and I am depressed." Unless he changes this belief, nothing will change.

Had he learned early in life that his thoughts and attitudes have a very direct influence on his circumstances, he would not be in this state now.

Fortunately, it is never too late. By gradually reconstructing the mind and training it to dwell on that which you have and want, rather than what you lack, you can begin to affect changes for the better.

Don't be concerned if these changes do not become evident immediately. You have planted the seeds, and that is all that is necessary. If you plant seeds in your garden you don't dig them up a few days later to see if they are germinating.

Know that you have set forces in motion and that everything you desire already exists for you. (A friend is only someone you have not met as yet.)

This is one of my favorite quotations: "There are no uninteresting things, there are only uninterested people."

The potential of interest, like that of happiness, is in our attitude to what we have, rather than to what we have not.

2

The Power of Love

The most powerful force in the world is love. At times its power is so great it is awesome.

Love is not a respector of time, space or place. In fact, the greatest manifestations of love I've seen have been in a hate-filled environment.

Those in unhappy circumstances have a greater opportunity to express love than those whose lives are void of problems. Perhaps this is the Law of Compensation.

I once spoke to a group of parents of handicapped children. During the evening a mother said that in the beginning she constantly asked the question, "Why did this have to happen to me?"

Finally the answer came to her: "So that you will know the true meaning of love." This person experienced a dimension of love that is denied most of us.

Any doubts I ever held concerning love's power came to an abrupt halt several years ago. I was conducting a class at San Quentin Prison, and an argument was in progress.

I was trying to impress 75 convicts that love is more powerful than hate. Not one agreed with me.

One of the men was particularly vehement in his disagreement. His name was Norman, and he had been incarcerated for three years. His wife and two children lived in Seattle, and he had not not had a letter from her during that time.

During this period his hatred and resentment for her festered, and he spend most of his waking moments plotting her murder upon his release.

When he heard me say that love was so powerful that it transcends time and space he really became aroused.

"If what you say is true," he growled, "you should be able to show me how to get a letter from my wife. I haven't heard from her since I've been here."

The other men grew silent, and Norman had a sarcastic grin on his face. By this time I had learned that if the teachings I presented to the convicts were to have any meaning, I had to face challenges such as this.

However, I also had the benefit of knowing that the teachings are infallible when put into practice.

"Let me ask you one question first," I said. "Was there ever a time when you and your wife were happy and in love with each other?"

Norman's expression, which always exuded hate, changed immediately. "Yes, he answered, "the first few years were fine, and our family was a happy one."

"All right," I said, "if you will do exactly as I say I believe you will receive a letter from her. For the next two weeks your every thought must be concentrated upon those happy times. Whenever you think of your wife and children it must be with thoughts of love. Refuse to entertain any thoughts of hatred or revenge."

7

Norman reluctantly agreed to attempt the experiment.

When I returned for another visit two weeks later I hardly recognized Norman. He looked peaceful, and his perpetual frown had disappeared. He had a letter in his hand.

He tried to read it to the group, but became too emotional. He asked me to read it for him, which I did with difficulty.

When I finished, I doubt if there was a dry eye in the room, including mine. I still remember it almost word for word.

"Dear Norman," it began. "I hope you will forgive me for not writing for so long. A strange thing happened a few days ago. I remembered all the happy times we had together, and I was overwhelmed by a feeling of love for you. The children and I want you back and we are waiting for you."

Recently I received another letter from Don, an ex-convict who had been brought up in an environment filled with hate. He has now been free for several years and has purchased a new home for his family.

He writes:

"It was only when I re-entered my old environment and tried to re-establish old relationships that the change in myself became apparent. I could no longer relate to my former companions; we were as strangers. They went back to their life of crime and I went back to my family

"My hate put me in prison and my lack of hate is keeping me out. Strange how people look all of their lives for something to make them happy when all they have to do is rid themselves of their negative emotions and they find that happiness was there all the time.

"I can now see hate in others just as you saw it in me years ago in those cold walls of Folsom Prison. You were right when you told me I had to forgive everyone and learn to love in order to overcome my hate."

"We have Faith, Hope, and Love; these three. And the greatest of these is Love."

3

Dispense With 'If Onlys'

"If only I had done differently."

"If only this had never happened."

"I wish I had never done that."

Almost all of us have at least one incident in the past we would like to eradicate or change. We accept the fact that this is impossible and so live with the subsequent feelings of guilt and/or regret.

This is not necessarily true. (Not that we can demand a replay or second chance.) However we are given the opportunity — which may be just as effective — of altering our viewpoint concerning past events in our lives.

Consider, if you can, that maybe what you did or left undone was not as bad as you thought it was. Perhaps early conditioning caused beliefs to become deeply ingrained in your mind that were false.

As long as you hold onto them, they are true, as far as you are concerned. It is these beliefs concerning what happened that are victimizing you more than the event itself.

For example, think back to your school days. You received a poor grade in math, and were informed you were lazy and stupid. You were too immature to rationalize that perhaps you failed because the teacher did not explain the subject clearly, so you accepted this evaluation of yourself as being true.

Our beliefs concerning the past have a very definite influence upon our present life. If they are of a negative nature, we can, with reflection and understanding, change them.

It is not easy, however. You may have become "labeled" and so you are acting in a manner which serves to reinforce these beliefs about yourselves, even though false.

Thus, those who think of themselves as being unpopular and without friends will act accordingly. Their thoughts of the past will always be focused on the negative aspects of their lives, and so they will continue to be friendless.

This can all be changed if they would recall the positive things they have done and concentrate upon those instead.

Control of one's thoughts is tremendously effective in all areas of life. Unfortunately, when one has a set opinion, any suggestion or idea that is contrary to that opinion is likely to go unnoticed.

For example, a person has an aversion to airplane travel because of fear. A plane crashes and this reinforces the fear. "Just as I told you," he or she says, "it is unsafe to travel by air."

Forgotten are the thousands of planes that take off and land safely every hour of every day. Also overlooked are the train and car accidents that happen frequently.

This person is in the same category as one who recalls only the negative aspects of his or her life.

There is much unfairness and cruelty in the world. Many people have a poor self-image and a low opinion of themselves which is unwarranted.

Parents and others frequently demean and belittle children, perhaps unknowingly, with lasting results.

Many so-called overweight people are prime examples of this injustice.

They have long been conditioned to believe that the only reason they are overweight is that they are weak and lack will-power. New scientific facts are emerging proving that this is not necessarily true.

Obese people, it is being discovered, have a different body chemistry than others, and it is not always an absence of will-power that is the cause of the problem.

In the meantime, however, the damage has been done. Their belief in this false concept concerning the cause of their being overweight has lowered their self-esteem, and they subconsciously eat more to reinforce it.

This may sound like a paradox, but I know from experience that we all are inclined to live up to the expectations of others, whether that expectation be high or low.

I have known many ex-convicts who have avoided committing crimes which would have resulted in their being returned to prison for the sole reason that a few people believed in them.

Conversely many have returned to prison because no one believed in them or expected them to stay out. The principle of living up to others' expectations of us is applicable to all.

Placing too much attention upon a problem is not conducive to solving it. Taking the mind off the problem entirely and choosing a positive aspect of one's life to concentrate upon instead may be more effective.

Concentrate upon your good points, of which you have many.

It has been said that even God cannot change the past. You, however, can change your reaction to the events of the past.

4

See Beyond 'What Is'

Those who have the ability to see beyond "what is" have a tremendous advantage over those who do not have this ability.

It enables them to see the potential in any given situation, instead of accepting the "status quo" as being permanent.

This applies to one's personal life as well as to situations. Being able to see yourself as you could be gives you the incentive to take steps that would result in your becoming that person.

If you cannot perceive of yourself as being any different in the future, it is highly unlikely you will ever be any different.

It is easy to develop a defeatist attitude concerning our potential for a better life, believing an improvement is dependent upon outside forces. When we refuse to take the responsibility ourselves, no improvement is likely in our circumstances.

To overcome the tendency to depend upon others, begin by making a list of the changes you could make in your life by relying solely on your own efforts. If you are honest with yourself, the list will be surprisingly extensive.

This will be a great step forward but it could also be a little traumatic. You will no longer be able to indulge in self-pity, because you will realize you are responsible to a large degree for your current circumstances

I once knew a young man who was always bemoaning the fact that he was very frail. I told him to stop thinking of himself as he was but to visualize himself as he might be if he were to meet certain conditions. One of the conditions was to "pump iron" or lift weights every day. Being able to form the mental picture of himself as he could be gave him the incentive to meet the conditions. He became the robust person he had always wanted to be without outside help of any kind.

The alcoholic or drug addict sees himself as he is and loses hope. He should attempt to see himself as he would be without the addiction and hold that picture in his mind at all times. Eventually, he will change to correspond to the picture he has formed.

You will be easily discouraged if you insist upon placing limits upon what you can do or become. There is much more to you than the person you now perceive. You may be making the mistake of judging yourself by outer appearances only. There is a vast inner world which consists of your thoughts and your beliefs. Concentrate upon changing this inner world first.

Don't see yourself as you are but as you could be. Then take the first step toward that objective. It may seem impossible to the person you are now, but don't contrast the one you are now with the one you want to be.

Someone once said to me, "There is a position I desire very much, but I could never fill it." He went on to explain that it required a great deal of public speaking, at which he professed to be a complete flop. "I agree with you that it would be impossible to fill the position as you are now," I said, "but it is a cop-out to believe you must forever remain that way. No one is unchangeable." I literally dragged him to a Toastmasters meeting. He became a regular member and, within a few months, turned into a capable speaker. He then obtained the position which had been out of reach for the person he once was.

Many people have latent talents but are unwilling to admit it, even to themselves. After all, if they admitted they have talents they might feel obligated to do something to develop them!

There is one requisite to effecting a change for the better in your life. It is faith, and a belief in your own power of accomplishment. This is not so much faith in yourself as you are now; rather it is faith in your potential. If you have this, your success is assured. Without it, many of your goals will remain beyond your reach.

The Bible says, "Faith is the substance of things hoped for, the evidence of things not seen." This is the definition of true faith! Concentrate on the vast areas of your mind that are still untapped. Permit your mind to become receptive. Ideas will flow in, and you will be led to act. Have faith that the result you want is within your realm of accomplishment, and it will be. You are constantly making a pattern of yourself by your beliefs about yourself. This pattern determines the quality of your outer world. It is within your power to change.

5

New Ideas from Old Proverbs

As I pointed out in recent articles, some of the greatest wisdom is contained in a single sentence or a solitary thought. In fact, teachers of olden times preferred to present their students with one concept at a time, and have them meditate upon it to the exclusion of all else.Only until the teacher was satisfied that the subject had been thoroughly absorbed and understood were they permitted to go on to another.

Since those articles appeared, several people have told me they have attained a new level of understanding by using this method of learning. Here are a few more, followed by my comments. Your interpretation of the quotation might be entirely different and will be much more important to you than mine would be. You will be amazed at the thoughts that will come to you as you meditate on each for a period of time. You might even want to write them down and add to them occasionally. Unfortunately, I am not always able to give credit to the author.

"Most frustrations are the result of the individual knowingly or unknowingly assuming a mold or pattern which is imposed upon him from an outside source."

It is strange how we permit ourselves, perhaps unconsciously, to conform to the expectations of others. Sometimes, of course, it goes even deeper than that. There are instances where people are literally forced to behave in a manner against their will. Frustration is the natural result. When we act contrary to our inner feelings and beliefs, a conflict is created. Those involved are seldom aware of the cause of their frustrations, so they are difficult to overcome. What might be called mental arthritis sets in. This can be worse than muscular arthritis. When one's thoughts become rigid and not open to change he or she lives within an invisible circle from which there is no escape.

We need not and should not act to conform to the labels others place upon us if it is contrary to our nature.

"Your world is a projection of you."

This is difficult for some to accept. This is particularly true of those who believe we have little or no control over our lives. However, upon reflection, it becomes easily apparent at least to some degree. It is said the nature of our thoughts and our general attitude toward life create an "energy field" which surrounds us.

We all know people who lift us up by their mere presence. Others cause us to become depressed. It is not so much what they say or do but what they seem to project that makes the difference. When one is beset by worries and doubts concerning his ability plus fear of the future, one loses his magnetic attraction.

This is why you find it difficult to respond to a person in this mood. You feel "down" yourself when in his or her presence. On the other hand, the optimistic person has a positive aura surrounding him and all of life seems to respond in kind.

A piece of steel which is magnetized can lift many times its own weight. If it is not magnetized, it cannot lift anything — even the weight of a feather. It is the same with people. Others are literally compelled to respond to you in direct relationship to your inner beliefs about yourself. There is another similar quotation, I think, by the Greek philosopher Hermes: "Your world is an outer manifestation of your inner thoughts and attitudes. As within, so without."

"Freedom of speech and freedom of action are meaningless without freedom to think."

During the last few years we have gained almost unlimited latitude of our speech and actions. Unfortunately, this has somehow diminished our ability to think. Too much freedom in one area detracts from freedom in another. Because there are fewer restrictions, addiction to alcohol, drugs and tobacco is becoming more prevalent. The addicted persons have lost their ability to think rationally, and no longer have freedom of choice. For example, the alcoholic can no longer enjoy an occasional drink.

When you are free to do what you want, you may lose your freedom to do as you like!

6

Change Beliefs About Yourself

I am convinced that many of our problems are of our own making. I also believe that almost without exception, the solution to our problems is within our power to find.

Many persons inform me that they are concerned about their inability to overcome harmful habits.

"I find it impossible to break this habit," they say. This statement is an almost certain indication that they will fail. Habits are indeed hard to break. They are much easier to discard.

There is a big difference between the two approaches, and this should be recognized. Attempting to break a habit requires an act of will. Discarding something and replacing it with something else requires much less effort or willpower. "Instead of doing that, I will do this," you tell yourself. Decide what it is you wish to eliminate from your life. Whatever it is, tell yourself, "I now choose to do something else instead."

It is your choice; therefore, it does not require willpower. You are not giving up anything; you are merely replacing it. The void that will be left will be filled with something of your own choosing.

It is essential that you develop a replacement before dropping the habit.

For example, if you have been devoting several hours a day to television, decide what you will do with those hours when you stop watching it. Or if you always drink before lunch or dinner, do something else during that period. Writing, reading, meditating, or exercising are a few suggestions.

One's mental attitude concerning the discarding of a habit is important. This well eventually determine its success or failure. You alone can determine your mental attitude. If you decide to let a cigarette, a piece of pie, or a drink have power over your life, be honest and don't blame someone else.

Another conclusion I have formed is that, as a general rule, people don't expect good things to happen to them. I know this because they are usually surprised when something good does happen. They write, "I tried following one of the principles outlined in your articles and I was amazed at the wonderful results!"

Why should they be surprised? Too many have an air of pessimism and gloom. If good fortune does strike, they find it difficult to accept. "This is too good to be true," they say, and so it is not long before whatever they gain is lost. "I'm a $200,000-a-year salesman," a man wrote. "Others in the company reach and surpass that figure, but my volume is always the same. Why is this and what can be done?"

He had unknowingly answered his first question. *You are what you think*, and he thought of himself as a $200,000-a-year salesman. He pinned a label on himself.

The solution involved only a few steps. He was to think of himself as a $300,000-a-year salesman and to act the part.

It is necessary to perform an act of faith, so I suggested he buy some clothes befitting a successful salesman. Next, he was to construct in his mind an event which would take place when he reached his goal. He chose to picture himself receiving the prize for best salesman at his company's annual banquet. He did this daily. Finally, as he made each call, he was to assume the feeling and attitude he would have if he had already made several consecutive sales, regardless of whether it were true.

The story has a strange and sad ending. He followed the required steps and attained his goal. He actually did receive the highest award at the annual banquet. He wrote me that he just could not believe it! The following year, however, his volume dropped to its previous level of $200,000. Apparently his beliefs about himself had never really changed. Lip service won't effect the change. Willpower alone is not permanently effective. Unless a change occurs within your nature, your true beliefs concerning yourself will manifest themselves in your life.

The picture we habitually hold of ourselves is far smaller than it could be, so change the picture.

7

An Experience to Remember

When I was in my mid-twenties, I had a strange experience. I've hesitated to write about it because I felt not many persons would believe it really happened. I decided to tell about it now because, during the last few years, I have encountered many people who have lost hope and faith in the future. I am confident that the few words uttered by a stranger whom I met for only a brief moment will be as meaningful to them as they have been for me.

This is the story: At that particular time, it became mandatory, if I were to keep my job, that I take a trip from California through Southern Oregon. The only transportation I had was a dilapidated old Plymouth that had long ago seen its best days. Its brakes were virtually nonexistent, and it used almost as much oil as it used water, and this was considerable. The most speed I could coax from it was 35 miles an hour. If the groaning of the engine was any indication, even that modest speed imposed great strain on its every part.

In spite of these handicaps, I took off one stormy morning in early November. By the third day, with the storm growing in intensity rather than abating, the car was almost as wet inside as it was outside.

It was at this point that the following strange, unexplainable events occurred. I was chugging along a lonely road, approaching the Oregon border. The wind was howling, and the rain was a deluge. Visibility was almost zero, and the embattled engine chose this unpropitious moment to give up the ghost and die!

I was able to coast to a place a few feet off the highway and sat there quietly bemoaning my fate. I calculated I was at least 30 miles from the next town, and nightfall wasn't far off.

Suddenly, I glimpsed through the rearview mirror the headlights of a vehicle approaching behind me. I was surprised, because I hadn't seen another car for the last several hours. I didn't think anyone in his right mind would venture forth in weather such as this!

The car stopped behind me, and I was more than a little apprehensive. Still, I think I was more glad than afraid, because I realized that if my situation were to improve, I must have outside help.

A tall man, whom I could barely see because of the elements, came to my window. I rolled down the window and tried to make myself heard above the wind and the driving rain. "The engine died," I shouted. He moved to the front of the car and raised the hood. I marveled that he was able to keep his balance against the force of the storm. He reached in and adjusted something — I never knew what — then signaled me to turn on the ignition.

To my amazement, the engine turned over. "I was afraid it had failed for the last time," I shouted. "Every car has at least one more start in it if given the proper attention," he hollered back.

All of a sudden, the wind grew quiet. The gale-force wind died down, and the rain turned to a drizzle. "The same principle applies to people," the stranger said softly. "Someday you will have occasion to apply this knowledge. Remember that as long as a single spark remains, it is not too late either for a car or a human being to make a fresh start." His words held little meaning to me at the time. I thanked him profusely and continued on my way. Incidentally, my old car never faltered again for the remainder of the trip.

Who was this man, and why did he stop and help an utter stranger on a lonely road? How did he happen to come along just at that particular moment? How was he able to start my car so easily?

It was 25 years before I was to realize the significance of those strange events. I was being taken on a tour of Folsom Prison before starting my first class. After seeing the hopeless expression on the faces on many of the men, I mentally despaired of being able to help. Suddenly, my mind bridged a quarter of a century, and I heard the words of the stranger as plainly as when they were uttered:

"Every car has the power to start once more if given the proper attention. The same principle applies to people. As long as a single spark remains, it is not too late either for a car or a person to make a fresh start. Someday you will have occasion to apply this knowledge."

8

Avoid Making Comparisons

The world would be a better place, I think, if one word were eliminated from our vocabulary. That word is "compare," with all its variations.

Here are two dictionary definitions of the word which make this point evident: "To be as good as . . . " "To bring together for the purpose of noting points of likeness and difference."

This word is responsible for countless thousands of people living with a poor self-image. Finding yourself constantly compared with someone else begins when you commence school, at the very latest. If you have been blessed with older brothers and sisters, it may start before you learn to talk or walk.

"Why can't you be a good little boy like your brother?" "Why can't you get an 'A' in algebra as your sister did?" "Your brother was a star football player, and you refuse even to try!"

Before long, either consciously or unconsciously, we start comparing ourselves with others and end up feeling inferior.

Completely overlooked is the fact that it is quite natural that we should be less proficient in some areas of life. That, however, does not classify us as failures. As Will Rogers once said, "We are all ignorant, but about different things." To compare one person with another is cruel and unjust.

Furthermore, there is no logic to it. It is a well-known and accepted scientific fact that no two persons who ever lived were exactly alike. That alone should prove the futility and unfairness of comparison. Of course, this works both ways. If it is unfair to compare yourself with, or to be compared unfavorably with others, it is equally wrong to compare yourself favorably.

Although you may excel in some areas of life, so will you fall short in others. The same holds true for everyone, so why make comparisons at all? Everyone is born with certain aptitudes which may have nothing to do with heredity. Many believe these aptitudes are hold-overs from past lives.

This theory would explain why some have to work hard to become proficient at something, while others become proficient with very little effort. If this theory is true, it is one more reason to avoid making comparisons.

It is easy to misjudge the value of someone's contributions to a cause. This mistake frequently happens in tne world of sports. All the other players take a back seat to the one who hits a home run in the 10th inning. Overlooked is the batter who skillfully executed a sacrifice bunt in an earlier inning to advance a runner, who then scored on a single. If it were not for this virtually unnoticed effort, the game would have been lost and there would not have been a 10th inning. In the eyes of the casual spectator however, there was no comparison between the two efforts. The home-run hitter was the hero of the game.

There are few victories either in life or in sports that are won entirely by oneself. I was happy to read a description not long ago of a rarity in baseball, a no-run, no-hit game. The writer of the article, while giving due credit to the pitcher, also rightfully praised the catcher and fielders. He implied that all the players had a part in the victory, and this of course is true.

There is another point to consider when making comparisons. One person may be doing quite well by the world's standards but still be performing far below his potential.

Another person, although his performance is greatly below that of the former, may be doing his best. In the final judgment, I believe the latter's performance will be rated as the higher.

When you compare yourself with others, you are being unfair to yourself. You may become so discouraged you will never attempt to reach your full potential. And yet the person with whom you are being compared performed exactly as you are doing when he was in your stage of development. With the same amount of training and aptitude, you probably could do as well — if not in this particular area, then in another. When you eliminate the fear of comparisons, you will be amazed at your accomplishments.

9

Concentrate on Solution — Not Problem

A compass, no matter how accurate, won't help you find your way unless you know where you are now. It is a mistake to set goals and start projects before doing some self-appraising.

Ask yourself, "Where am I now in relation to where I want to go? How am I now compared with the way I want to be?" This kind of thinking will give you a much better perspective. The person wishing to lose weight, for example, should be specific: "I now weigh 140 pounds and in six months I wish to weigh 120 pounds." This statement is much more effective than vaguely, saying, "I think I'll try to lose some weight."

A longing for more money and possessions won't produce results, but a strong desire for specific amounts will. The first step should always be to evaluate your present status. When you have done this, it will be easier to envision the fulfillment of your goals.

Many persons with whom I have talked feel that the realization of a goal is dependent upon something someone else must do. Instead, they must be dependent on themselves and their own actions.

It is far better to start right where you are now, then decide what areas of your life could be improved without outside help of any kind.

For example, your losing the desired amount of weight will ultimately depend on *your* eating less, not upon someone else eating less, as attractive as this sounds.

There are thousands of people who feel their lives are hopeless and without meaning. Before a change for the better can take place, they will need to get rid of the false belief that they cannot do anything about improving the situation themselves. They must learn that everything they do causes a reaction of some kind. Therefore, if one constantly thinks and acts in a negative way, he cannot expect anything but negative results.

As soon as one accepts this Law of Cause and Effect, his world begins to change. He realizes that, if it works in negative ways, it must also work in positive way.

He will arrive at the conclusion that there is meaning to his life after all, because he has control over his circumstances. There is no further need to rely on what someone else may or may not do.

Of course, it is much easier to blame our lack of accomplishments on others instead of taking responsibility ourselves. Refuse to accept the premise that you are powerless to effect changes in your life. These changes won't take place, however, until your own attitudes and actions change. If you insist on depending upon others, you could wait a lifetime. Many make the mistake of allowing their problems to absorb most of their attention and energy.

Those in debt think constantly about their debts. If they are ill and in pain, their minds are occupied with thoughts of sickness and pain. Any unwanted condition in their lives dominates their thoughts.

This situation is understandable, but it is not the best way to overcome these conditions.

There are simple stories told in the Old Testament, and they may have a deeper meaning than is apparent. Perhaps some of the teachings were given in this manner so they could be easily understood by everyone. One such story is that of Daniel in the lion's den.

Daniel was locked in the den with several lions which had been purposely starved for the occasion. If this had been you or I, I'm sure we would have placed our entire attention upon the lions. Not Daniel, however!

There was a light coming into the den from above. It was upon this light that he placed his entire concentration as he prayed, and he was saved. According to the interpretations of this story by the late Emmet Fox, a noted author and lecturer for many years, the lions represented problems such as we all face at times.

The light represented freedom to Daniel, or the solution to his immediate problem. By turning his attention away from the problem and focusing instead upon the solution, he was saved. The lions (or problems) lost their power to harm him.

Most of us set goals, then think of all the obstacles that stand in the way of our achieving them. By concentrating upon the "light," or solution, instead of upon the problems, the obstacles become as harmless as did the lions in the story of Daniel.

George Willig, the famed mountain climber, said this about overcoming fear:

"Block out all thoughts of falling from your mind and place your attention upon your destination."

10

Discard False Beliefs About Aging

New scientific discoveries indicate that before too long it may be possible to reverse the aging process.

Some of the nation's top flight researchers who are studying this field met not long ago in Tucson, Ariz., with executives in the insurance industry. These executives were told to expect some major break throughs in the next few years. Not only do the scientists expect to be able to prolong life but also to improve the quality of life for older people. They expect to increase the average life-span by many years. Insurance companies are not taking this news lightly.

Dr. Alex Comfort, a gerontologist and a fellow of the Institute for Higher Studies and a recognized spokesman for research into aging, said:

"We are gradually getting away from the view that there is an 'aging process' and more to the idea that there is a computer that controls life-span. The computer, which involves as few as 1,000 cells, lies in the brain, and the task at hand now is to try and reset its 'clock.'"

It is also said that it well be possible to take a pill to improve your brain output and to keep your head and mind free from the ravages of growing old. There are many, I'm sure, who will not be ready for this apparent good news. Aside from the obvious problems which would arise, such as unemployment, over-population, and so on, there are others.

The psychological aspects loom every bit as great. One's entire outlook on life might have to be altered. Being "too old" is a timeworn excuse not to do many things that might be beneficial to oneself, as well as to others. "I'm too old to start painting or writing or to do volunteer work," people say. This excuse may no longer be valid. "There wouldn't be any sense in quitting smoking at my age," I've heard many older persons say. Soon they may have to think up another excuse for not stopping. If they can conceivably live another 60 or 70 years, why live them in poor health?

An excuse for not performing as well as others is treasured by some people, as incongruous as this may appear. The person married to an alcoholic who stops drinking, for example, is not always as happy as one would expect. No one feels sorry for the person anymore.

The opportunity to indulge in self-pity is also lost. Often, the result is divorce and another marriage to a person with similar problems. Looking at the positive side of a longer, healthier life, however, we see many benefits.

For many, it will mean a second chance to do the things they had always wanted to do but somehow never found the time. For others, it will give a deeper meaning to their personal relationships. Knowing that many years may remain for both persons, perhaps they will make a greater effort to keep their relationship happy.

What will be the attitude of the young if longevity becomes a reality? Will they make the most of it and

34

develop their talents to the limit, or will they feel that, so long as there is so much time, the necessity for immediate effort does not exist?

Even if none of the expectations of the scientists regarding aging come true, there is something each individual can do.

We can rid ourselves of the delusion that we are old because we have lived a certain number of years. This is a false assumption, but, so long as we believe it, it is true for us. We believe what we have been conditioned to believe, without forming our own opinions. All that really counts is how you feel right now. If you don't feel active and vital now, it makes no difference whether you are 20 or 70.

Ask yourself what you can do to change your condition now. Begin by changing your mental attitude. Discard the belief that your chronological age should affect the way you feel. Then decide what needs to be done to make you feel better and become more active. Your physical body must change to correspond to your new mental attitude.

You are as young as you feel and you do have the power to change the way you feel. It may be earlier than you think!

11

Favorite Quotations

Here are some more of my favorite quotations.

The first is by the renowned American psychologist, William James. *"If you would be rich, you will be rich; if you would be good, you will be good, if you would be learned, you will be learned. Wish then, for one thing exclusively and not for a hundred other incompatible things just as strongly."*

Most of us, I'm afraid, do just the opposite.

We wish for many things and so don't put forth concentrated effort on any one. The years go by and we wonder at our lack of accomplishments. Far better to decide on the one thing we want the most and stay with it until it is ours. Then, and only then, should we go on to the next goal.

There is no stopping the person who knows what he wants and is willing to put forth the effort to attain it. Furthermore, he receives an unexpected bonus. His capacity for enjoyment is far greater than those who flounder through life without a purpose. Those who spend most of their time looking for ways to avoid work so as to have more leisure time are usually too tired to enjoy it!

Someone said, *"There are two things to aim for in life. First is to get what you want, and, after that, to enjoy it. Only the wisest achieve the second."*

American author Bruce Barton said: *"What a curious phenomenon it is that you can get people to die for the liberty of the world who will not make the little sacrifice that is needed to free themselves from their own individual bondage."*

Another writer named Emmons adds: *"Habit is either the best of servants, or the worst of masters."*

It is easier to dispose of unwanted habits if you control your attitude regarding them. If you think of a bad habit as something that is making you a slave you should be more willing to drop it. Most take the opposite viewpoint, and regard the disposing of a bad habit as giving up something of value. As Barton points out, we are unwilling to make the relatively small sacrifice that would grant us freedom.

No one can be free without practicing a certain amount of self-discipline. (Self-discipline should be thought of as a form of freedom instead of regarding it as self-denial. This is very important.)

Each time one resists indulging in a bad habit, the easier it is to resist it the next time. Eventually no more resistance will be needed, and the person becomes free. It is the self-discipline at the beginning that leads to eventual freedom and increased enjoyment of life.

Another quote, I'm not sure by whom: *"Discontent is the penalty we must pay for not being grateful for what we have."*

37

There is one sure cure for discontent. Pretend you lost everything you have, then got it all back again. If one is not grateful for what he has, it usually means he or she is evaluating his possessions according to what others have. If this is habitual, discontent will become a permanent part of this person's nature. There will always be someone with more than he in some area. There is one way I know that will ensure a richer, more fulfilling existence. This is to increase your contributions to life. In the long run one's rewards will not exceed one's contributions.

Unfortunately, this is the last thing to enter the discontented person's mind. Most of the footprints left in the sands of time have been made by work-shoes! The writer Walpole said, *"People are often capable of greater things than they perform. They are sent into the world with bills of credit, and seldom draw to their full extent."* There are few to whom this does not apply, and it is a great cause of discontent. Deep within us is the knowledge that we could do better if we would put forth a little more effort.

The next step is to start making excuses. The phrase "I could have done better if only" is usually followed by a list of reasons why we no longer try. This may lead to all sorts of indulgences which help us compensate for our failures.

Few, if any of us, will live up to our full potential in this lifetime.

There is a method, however, that will help us along the way. Make a mental picture of the ideal "you," or the way you would like to be. By holding that picture of yourself in your mind at all times you will find you will act in the ways that will objectify your image.

12

'Victim of Circumstances' Ignores Inner Resources

People become depressed because they believe they no longer have control over their lives.

They have permitted themselves to become the victims of circumstances and thus feel helpless. Although outside help is sometimes required, it is best to look within oneself for the answer. Unfortunately, being unaware of this fact, one usually looks there last. The basic premise, in my opinion, behind every great teaching is this:

We all have the God-given power to sustain us through every trial and tribulation, as well as to find the answer to every problem that confronts us. You may have fallen into the habit of saying, "I can't do this" or, "I don't have the strength to see me through."

That may be true, except for one factor. You are selling yourself short. You have a vast amount of inner resources which you have allowed to remain untapped. When you learn to call upon them, many self-imposed limits will be removed. It will be like living in a different world.

Most of the great feats of history were performed in this manner. They appeared to be "superman" efforts, but in reality the person simply used the power that was already his. Everyone of us is capable of much more than we have shown. Having been conditioned to believe in our limitations, we accept them as fact.

In many cases, all that is necessary to regain control over one's life is to follow a few basic principles. After all, it is not a healthful or happy feeling to be at the mercy of whatever happens or to be subject to the whims of others.

To dispel this sense of inadequacy, you must realize that your own thoughts and actions have played a large part in determining your present circumstances. Perhaps you will need to prove this truth to yourself. Begin by accepting the fact that you have the freedom to choose how you will react to any situation that may arise in your life.

It is very difficult to convince people of this fact. We have been so conditioned to respond in certain ways to situations that it never occurs to us that alternatives exist. We may not be able to change the events but we can try very hard to change our reactions to them. Here is a method taught almost a century ago by Annie Besant, an educator and founder of the Theosophical Society:

Choose a situation that is very irritating to you and one that happens fairly frequently. Picture yourself going through this situation calmly. Do this often. When the situation does arise, you will find you will be able to face it without your previous irritation. The more ways we can discover to control our reactions, the more serene our lives will become.

A basic knowledge of the Law of Cause and Effect is helpful. This principle says that nothing happens by chance and that every effect has a cause behind it. Immediately, many will bring to mind a happening in their lives for which it would be difficult to find a valid cause.

Nevertheless, it should become readily apparent that we could become a "causer" instead of becoming the "effect" of our environment, our early conditioning, and the will of others.

It is possible to respond to people rather than react to them. If someone makes a disparaging remark to you, instead of reacting, try responding with a smile or a change of subject. It's surprising how easy it is to turn an unpleasant situation around.

As this was written, we are faced with long lines at the gas stations. You must choose whether to react or to respond. You can become impatient and upset or use the time to catch up on reading or your correspondence. The point is that the choice is yours. No one can make it for you.

We must strive to reach the stage where our happiness is not entirely dependent upon what happens or upon the actions of others. If you expect others always to conform to your wishes, you are obviously doomed to disappointment.

Perhaps we should adopt the philosophy that life is a series of experiences, one after the other. Good or bad, pleasant or unpleasant, they will all pass.

13

Dangerous to Make False Assumptions

When something unexpected happens, either in business or in our daily lives, our natural reaction is to form an opinion concerning the result.

We assume we know what the outcome will be, so we proceed accordingly. Our entire course of action will be based on our assumption being correct. But what if it isn't? Owners and managers of businesses are constantly faced with this dilemma. Outside conditions, over which they have no control, suddenly change.

An opinion must be formed as to what the reaction of the public will be to the new conditions. This opinion or assumption should not be formed hastily. The attitude off all the employees will be vitally affected, as they will reflect the beliefs of the boss.

If one's mind is focused on the negative aspects only, the positive ones may never be recognized and could be overlooked entirely.

A case in point is the gasoline shortage. Because of it, manufacturers and sellers of larger cars apparently are assuming the public will no longer want their product. It could be that their assumption is wrong. However, it really won't make any difference. With all their attention focused in that direction, their assumption will help assure the result they expect. They are assuming they can read the public's mind, and this assumption can be dangerous in business.

It is possible that the majority of drivers are more interested in the number of miles their car will travel on a tankful of gas than the miles it will go on a gallon. Some, it seems reasonable to assume, would prefer a car with a tank that holds 20 or more gallons over one which holds 10 or less because of the longer distances driven between fill-ups. If looked at from this perspective, the gasoline shortage should spur the sales of larger cars rather than deter them. Looking for the positive aspect of any situation prevents one from becoming the victim of circumstances over which he has no control.

The morale of a business will rise and fall in direct proportion to that of management, and a company with low morale must eventually fail.

A few years ago, I wrote about a somewhat similar situation. The automobile business was in a slump as gas lines were long, and rumors of continuing shortages were rampant.

I met a car dealer I knew and asked him how his business was doing. "It's strange that you should ask that," he answered. "It's terrible with the other dealers, and it was terrible for me until recently. Now, however, it's great."

Seeing that I was curious as to what had caused the sudden change for the better, he told me this story:

"I have a sister in Tennessee whose husband is an accountant. He grew tired of that type of work and wanted to try his hand as a salesman. He was unable to find a position back there, and she asked me if I would let him sell cars for a few months. I agreed reluctantly. After the first month, his commission was greater than that of my other three salesmen's earnings combined!"

"He must have been a great salesman," I commented.

"Not at all," said the dealer. "His success lay in the fact that he didn't know any better. He didn't know people weren't supposed to be buying cars, so when someone entered the showroom, he assumed he or she came to buy. "My other salesmen assumed the person was only killing time, or that he just came to look, so they ignored him. No more, however, now they too are selling cars. They no longer hold preconceived opinions about anything."

One of the great tragedies is to look back over your life and discover how many times you have been the victim of false assumptions. The process starts when you are a very young child. You know that you are not as good-looking or as athletic as some, so you assume you will never be popular. This attitude may cause you to withdraw and not seek the friendship of others.

A well-meaning parent or teacher may inform you that you are not as bright as others and that you cannot expect much of yourself in the way of achievements. You assume they are correct, so you reason there is no use trying. If a child steals something, it could be because of a desire to be noticed. It may have been only a one-time act, but if the label of "thief" is pinned on him, he will most likely repeat it.

The world would be a better place in which to live if we assumed there is some good in every situation and in every person.

14

Recognize Your Power and Gain Control

One day I took a guest with me to speak to the group of men I met with each month at Folsom State Prison. Because he was a fine speaker and well-known teacher, I gave him free rein to take over the entire three hours. I sat over to the side.

This gave me my first opportunity to observe the convicts objectively and reflect on how or if they differed from those of us in the "free" world.

Some of these men I had known for a number of years. Folsom, being a maximum security prison, contains the so-called hard-core convicts. They are men who have been convicted at least three times and are serving long terms, many for life.

Several of the men in attendance that day had been coming to my class for more than 10 years. A few of the men were in their 30s, but most were much older. Although I always refrained from delving into their records, bits of information would emerge from our talks. I learned that some were victims of their passion for gambling, some for their inability to control their desire for drink or drugs, others had uncontrollable tempers.

Still, I conjectured, if you consider that everything is a matter of degree, this did not make them so much different from the rest of us. After all, most of us have some tendencies in those directions. There are few of us who do not, at times, over-indulge in one or the other of the so-called "vices."

Who among us has never had an almost uncontrollable urge to break something in a fit of anger or to strike out at someone? Others of us might rationalize that it is okay to cheat on our income tax, especially if we are sure we can get away with it. How did it happen, then, that these men reached the deplorable stage of having to spend their lives behind bars?

I began to observe them individually. I studied Marty, the gambler, while his attention was focused on the speaker. It was said that once he gambled his expensive home on the turn of a card and lost. His family deserted him after he turned to crime to support his addiction. At this very moment he was suffering because he had gambled away his last few cigarettes and had no money to replace them. Although he was past 50, I tried to visualize him as he might have been when a young boy.

Did his tragic life begin when he first started matching pennies? Most people gamble a little without such dire results. What was there about Marty that made him so different from the rest of us?

My gaze next rested on Joe, a nice looking fellow, convicted several times for armed robbery and numerous times for assault with a deadly weapon.

What was he like as a boy? I wondered.

Was the first time he stole a popsickle the beginning of the end? Most of us have done something similar without going on th greater crimes. Why and how was Joe different?

The next inmate was Art. This was a particularly sad case, because he was so brilliant.

Art had once worked his way up to a high executive position, then became the owner of a large business. He could handle every problem except the problem of his addiction to alcohol.

Gradually, according to his story, it took precedent over his lovely family and his business, and he lost them both. Art has told me that the only ambition he has left is to tell his story to every young person with a weakness for alcohol. He may never be granted that chance. He murdered a liquor store clerk for a quart of whisky. At that moment, the whisky meant more to him than a human life.

Before the day was over, I reflected on the wasted lives of many of the men present. Some of these men were regarded by criminal authorities as the most desperate criminals in the country. All of them, I knew, could have been leading happy, constructive lives in the free world instead of wasting their years in the living hell which is prison.

What was the difference between these men and others?

It was their refusal to accept the fact that every act must have a consequence.

We are free to choose what we do, but whatever we choose we must accept with it the subsequent inevitable resulting condition.

No one ever beat the Law of Cause and Effect. The laws of nature are changeless and irrevocable. As you sow, so shall you reap! Don't take my word for it. Art, Joe, Marty and thousands of others wasting their lives away in prison, are living examples.

15

Only Faith Can Release Your Power

Growth is synonomous with nature. Therefore, anything that remains stagnant is contrary to nature. This also applies to people and perhaps explains why those who have permitted themselves to live within a small circle experience frustration. This was explained by a writer named Ashley Montagu. *"The deepest personal defeat suffered by human beings is constituted by the difference between what one was capable of becoming and what one has in fact become."*

I'm sure this is true because I've seen what happens to those who make a sincere effort to start living up to their potential. The personality change that takes place is amazing.

Unfortunately, this does not happen very frequently. "What one has in fact become" indeed becomes an accepted way of life. As the years go by, this defeatist attitude becomes deeply cemented in the person's consciousness. That is probably the reason the rate of recidivism for convicts is so high. It never occurs to them that another way of life is possible.

Most of us feel that we are capable of more than we have shown, but don't take the necessary steps to change

49

the situation. The first requisite is to acknowledge that an improvement is possible in spite of appearances. This is difficult because habitual ways of thinking become deeply ingrained.

The picture one has of himself, his self-image, must be revised. As one's self-image is formed over a long period of time this can be a traumatic experience.

It is also important that one really wants an improvement in his circumstances, and this is not always the case. To some a change, even though beneficial, is not wanted. The "status quo," though abhorred, somehow carries with it a certain degree of comfort.

Starting on a new path requires an effort of the will. If the distance between where you are now and where you would like to be appears too great, you may decide not to make the effort.

It won't seem nearly as unreachable if you realize you can get there by degrees. A hill may loom steep from a distance, but once the ascent is begun the journey is easier than previously imagined.

If nothing is done to alleviate the deep inner feeling of discontent that has resulted from one's reviewing his "might have beens" the results can be disastrous. Not liking himself as he is, the person might look for a chemical change. If he or she turns to drugs or alcohol as a panacea an entire life could be wasted.

To a great extent we determine our own future. If we have concluded that something is beyond our capabilities to achieve, it will be because we won't try.

The human brain has often been compared to a computer, although it is much more complex. As with the mechanical computer, information given out can only be based upon the in-put.

For example, the most advanced computer in existence is capable of performing amazing feats of intricate mathematics. However, if you ask it to answer only simple problems of addition and subtraction its potential will be wasted. The same principle applies to humans.

It becomes obvious that your self-image determines how your brain is programmed. If you continually tell yourself that you are inadequate and limited as to your accomplishments, your potential will be wasted as surely as was the computer's. Your mind has no alternative but to obey the instructions you give it.

Thinking of yourself as a failure will cause you to act as a failure. If you have programmed your brain to believe that anything more than you now have is unattainable, discard those false beliefs and become receptive to the possibility of personal growth.

Retaining a negative self-image will cause you to build an invisible fence around yourself created by your self-imposed limits. Even if you manage to succeed temporarily, you will find ways to fail.

Only faith can release the tremendous power everyone possesses. Without faith this power lies dormant because it is not called upon.

Work your imagination overtime. If you can dream it you can attain it. Shakespeare said, *"We know what we are, but know not what we may be."*

16

Never Too Late for Atonement

All too frequently memories of one's mother leave one with a feeling of regret. This is especially true for those of us whose mother is no longer with us.

We think of the phone calls we could have made, the letters we neglected to write, the times we should have visited her but didn't.

This is another of life's situations which many falsely believe is beyond redemption. I've learned that life is not so cruel that it will not offer at least some degree of hope no matter what the circumstance. This may be difficult to accept when death is a factor, but if one has a strong desire to atone, not even death can stand in the way.

In one of my early columns I was able to give an example of the goodness of life and it's willingness to grant another chance to those with a strong desire to rectify a mistake. It bears repeating because there must be many who did not read it.

It is the story of Paul, an inmate of Folsom Prison. Of all the people I have known throughout the years, none was more filled with remorse than was Paul. His depression had progressed to the point where he was almost a mental case. He had received much therapy through the years to no avail. One day he told me his story.

"My father left us when I was in my early teens," he began. "I lived alone with my mother who was a wonderful woman. She had always been an avid reader but was slowly losing her sight. "She would have liked me to stay home and read to her, but I didn't have time. I was running around with a gang, and staying home with my mother wasn't exciting enough for me."

"Finally, however, I decided to mend my ways. The gang was beginning to get into trouble with the law, and I could see where I was headed. I left my friends early one night and went home to read to my mother.

"I found her dead in her chair with an open book in her lap which I knew she was unable to see well enough to comprehend."

"That night is indelibly printed on my memory, and is one which I'll never be able to forget. I didn't care what happened to me after that, and I soon ended up in prison. "I would gladly give the rest of my life for the opportunity to spend one evening reading to my mother, but it's too late."

Paul's story touched me greatly, and I was at a loss for words. He seemed beyond any help I was capable of rendering. All I could think of was this, and I probably didn't say it with much conviction: "Paul, with such a strong desire to atone for your neglect of your mother, I'm sure that life, or God, will some day give you the opportunity."The months went by, and Paul was released after many years of his life had been wasted in prison. Two more years passed, and I had all but forgotten him. Then late one night I received a phone call from New York. It was Paul. "Doug," he said, "I remembered you lived in Danville, so I was able to get your number.

You were right, life, or God, did find a way to relieve me of my remorse."

"Driving through town a few weeks ago," Paul continued, "I happened to notice a sign saying Convalescent Home, and I felt compelled to stop and enter the building. There was a lady sitting at the desk, and I approached her.

"Is there anyone here who would like to be read to?" I asked. She looked at me in astonishment. "There is an elderly lady here who loves to read but is going blind. I'll take you to her."

"We entered a room where a woman was sitting with an open book on her lap. She handed it to me as if she had been expecting me, and I began to read. For the next few weeks I visited and read to her many times."

"The other night while I was reading I sensed a change had taken place. I looked up and saw that she had quietly passed away. For one fleeting moment she took on the likeness of my mother, and she was smiling. I blinked my eyes, and now she was once again the lady I had been visiting. Immediately all of the remorse I had suffered and the regrets I had felt for years disappeared. Your words while I was still incarcerated came back to me. 'If your desire to atone is so great, somehow you will be given the opportunity.' I knew my mother had forgiven me."

At this time neither Paul nor I had any idea his story would some day reach millions of people, because I had no thought then of writing a column.

I've lost track of Paul, but I'm sure both he and his mother would approve. If only a few benefit from their story, the years of their suffering will not have been meaningless.

17

How to Overcome Hopelessness

Although conditions are much different now, many persons today have the same attitude that we had nearly 50 years ago. Young people then also were filled with fears and doubts

It was during the Great Depression, and there were more than 13,000,000 people unemployed. This was at a time when the population was much smaller than it is now. Jobs were nearly impossible to find, even for college graduates. Many men who previously had enjoyed high positions were literally reduced to begging to feed their families, as there was no employment insurance in those days. Some, who had lost their life savings in the stock market crash, committed suicide.

An atmosphere of despair prevailed over the country. If you were to see pictures of the thousands standing in the "bread lines", you would see this hopelessness revealed in the expressions on their faces. Although these conditions do not exist today, there is just as much uncertainty now as there was then.

Runaway inflation and lack of confidence in our government have caused young people to have the same feeling of pessimism we suffered. In fact, they are saying the same things we said:

"I'll never have a good enough job so I can afford to get married. I'll never be able to afford a new car or a new home."

We felt trapped, as though we were the victims of circumstances over which we had no control. Many of us accepted defeat from the start, believing that the conditions were insurmountable. It is this defeatist attitude that must be overcome.

In my case, 25 years were to go by before I would realize that it is not necessary to give power to circumstances. Many more years were to pass before I finally was able to put this realization into practice. Many never did get over the feeling of helplessness they acquired. It was as if they built an invisible fence around themselves and never emerged from its boundaries.

Why place limits upon your accomplishments when you cannot be sure any exist? You may have been conditioned to believe there are things you are incapable of doing, but that does not mean this assumption is true.

If you think prevailing conditions have the power to force you into a life of mediocrity, you are selling yourself short. Unfortunately, however, if you believe it, that is what will happen. It is easy to fall into negative habits of thinking, especially regarding oneself. This tendency must be avoided at all costs. The mental image you hold concerning yourself and your general attitude toward the world will have an effect on everything that happens to you. If you do not think well of yourself, it is useless to expect others to think well of you.

Through years of working with men in prison, I have made this discovery: The difference between a person who is happy, well-adjusted, and successful and the one who is a failure in his and others' eyes is relatively small. Mainly, it concerns the way the person feels about himself. The failure has a low opinion of himself and does not believe his life can possibly change for the better unless outer circumstances change.

The successful person refuses to allow circumstance to control him, knowing that he has an inner power that can take dominion over whatever circumstances he faces.

Although this inner power is within everyone, it lies dormant unless called upon. Therefore, it is possible to go through an entire lifetime without knowledge of its existence. The men whose lives I have seen change dramatically did not accomplish this change by relying on forces outside themselves, but rather on forces within themselve.

Try to assume the state of mind that nothing is beyond your reach. Don't assume, or take for granted, that your capabilities are limited. You can do much more than you assume you can do but you will never know if you surround yourself with an invisible barrier composed of self-doubts.

Your self-image is extremely important. It forms the foundation of what you can expect from life and therefore determines to a great extent what you will receive.

18

Life is a Series of Choices

Many of our troubles are of our own making, as difficult as this may be for us to admit.

We expose ourselves to potential trouble by choosing to be in a certain place and, when trouble is the result, we are filled with self-pity. It all could have been avoided if we had chosen differently.

In my later years, I have heard many "tales of woe." I always have empathy with those who tell me their problems, but I don't always have sympathy for them. I have often been in the same position as they are now and I realize it was my own choice that put me there.

Sometimes it appears as though we almost do this deliberately. Many are not comfortable when things go too smoothly, because then there is nothing to complain about.

It gives one a feeling of security to be able to point out all the reasons why he is not able to show more results for his efforts. As I look back upon my life, I realize I was sometimes guilty of this mistake.

I recall one experience, for example, that might have

had tragic results. It could easily have been avoided if I had not made myself vulnerable in the first place.

When I was in my twenties, I traveled as a salesman through Northern California and Southern Oregon. My wife went with me until the birth of the first of our two sons, then I traveled alone. I enjoyed playing cards with friends and considered myself a good poker player. Sometimes while on the road, I became bored and looked for a game.

It was always in the worst part of town in the back of a cigar store or pool room. You must remember that I was much younger and at least a little more foolish than I am now. I gradually realized that my chances of winning were absolutely zero, but at least it was something to help pass the time.

One night, I found a game in Marysville, Calif., in the lower section of town. This was in the late thirties, during the depression. The stakes were low by present standards, but in those days were probably considered high. The other players were much older and more skillful than I, but on this particular night I was having phenomenal luck. One of the players had been losing heavily and, as a result, was in a surly mood. We were playing five-card stud. With one card remaining, I had three two's, one of which was "buried." The loser had two fours showing and kept raising me.

On the last card I was dealt another two, much to my suprise, and he was dealt another four. I might have worried about his having the winning hand with four fours but I had happened to catch a glimpse of one in the discard pile.

When the betting was over, I turned up my hole card, showing that I had four twos. He turned over his, which was a fourth four!

"That is impossible!" I shouted. "There is a four in the discard pile."

As I said that, I felt a heavy hand on my shoulder. I looked up and saw a man who appeared to me to be seven feet tall.

"Son," he said. "I think you had better leave. Otherwise, they might find a body in the river in the morning."

Needless to say, I took his advice and quickly left.

For days afterward, I felt sorry for myself. I had been deprived of some money that was rightfully mine, and wondered why such a terrible thing had happened to me. I completely forgot to be grateful for still being alive.

It was some time before I matured enough to be able to face myself. What was I doing in that environment in the first place? I had to admit it was strictly my own choice and I was solely responsible for anything that might have happened to me. After all, no one forced me to be there.

As it turned out, the whole experience was a wonderful lesson. I never played in a professional poker game again. As a consequence, I never faced a deck which contained five fours.

A convict once said to me, "All of my troubles were the result of my going into bars. Every time I entered one, I got into a fight and ended up in jail."

"What do you mean every time?" I asked him. He didn't understand my question, so I explained.

"I can understand your visiting bars once or twice after getting into trouble, but apparently you kept returning, even though you must have known the inevitable result. Did someone force you to continue placing yourself in this environment?"

"No one forced me," he answered. "I always went under my own power."

Eventually he got the point.

If trouble seems to be hounding you, it may be that you are choosing the wrong environment. As I pointed out earlier, many of our toubles are the results of choices we make and therefore could be avoided.

19

Tragic Waste of Human Energy

We are constantly being reminded of the energy being wasted, both by the country at large and within our own homes.

As important as this problem is, it is even more shocking to see human energy being wasted. One need only visit a prison regularly to become aware of this situation.

Thousands of men, some with brilliant minds and all capable of fulfilling some purpose in life, are milling around and doing nothing day after endless day.

There is one thing these men have in common, and it is shared by many from the outside world. They want more from life but don't believe they are capable of achieving it. Therefore, they hesitate to make the effort.

To ease their consciences, they pretend that they really didn't want it in the first place. Many hold this attitude, and it can easily become a way of life.

Giving an all-out effort doesn't seem to be as popular today as it was in the past. This is why few persons stand out above the rest. One would think a professional athlete in particular would give everything he has for the short time he is asked to perform, but this is not always the case.

No matter what field they are in, some persons find it easier to go along with the crowd rather than risk failure. They submerge themselves in mediocrity, where they will not be noticed.

Going all-out might mean subjecting themselves to ridicule from their more complacent friends. I have seen many people become motivated to make something of themselves and then go back into their shells because of the derisive attitudes of their peers.

Childhood memories are lasting. Failing to recite well or to answer questions correctly are events not easily forgotten.

The student learns to say, "I don't know," simply to avoid the embarrassment of another failure, even when he thinks he knows the answer. This habit can easily result in not trying in other areas, and another wasted life is in the making.

One way out of this rut is to find something to become enthusiastic about. One suggestion — and this works wonders — is to discover the power of your mind to change your life. "Become transformed by the renewing of your mind," the Bible says.

Once you start utilizing this power, you will never tire of it, because the possibilities are endless. You may never have considered that you do not have to accept your life as being unchangeable and that you are not destined to remain at your present level. Once you discover you have the power to change, you cannot help becoming excited.

Many want freedom to do as they wish. It is much more important and rewarding to find inner freedom.

This means taking control of your mind and discovering what you have been missing. The best place to start is to change your thoughts concerning yourself, if they have been of a negative nature.

This is important, because your actions are reflecting these thoughts. A poor opinion of yourself results in a lack of confidence, and you are reluctant to try something new.

Your actions are simply corresponding to your beliefs about yourself. Many of these beliefs are false and are probably the result of opinions forced upon you by others.

Accept the possibility that they may be false and force yourself to do something you formerly feared to try.

Form a mental picture of yourself as one who is full of confidence. Before long, this new self-image will be reflected in your actions, without conscious effort on your part.

You will discover that you have many of the traits you always wished were yours. They remained buried only because you allowed them to lie dormant.

Remember, your future will be the same as your past unless you do something to change it.

20

You Are Not Powerless

People who feel powerless to improve their lot in life and see no hope for a better future usually react in one of two ways: They will become passive and unable to think for themselves or will become aggressive and perhaps even violent.

As illustrations, I can cite two extreme cases. The thousands who found themselves in Nazi concentration camps acted for the most part in the former manner. Having no hope of changing their situation, they followed instructions without question, even walking into the gas chamber.

On the other hand, many persons in prison react in the opposite manner. Feeling powerless, they become frustrated and sometimes adopt violent behavior. They are aggressive and hostile, not only to those in authority but also to their fellow inmates. If one is placed in a position where the right to make even simple decisions is denied him, a person becomes resentful and believes aggression is the only alternative. He then resorts to violence, if only to prove to himself that he still has some jurisdiction over his circumstances.

I believe that those who persist in committing crimes must be shut off from society until they are willing to abide by its laws. Relieving a person of all responsibilities, however, will do little or nothing to rehabilitate him.

Although few of us will ever face these extreme circumstances, many are in situations where they consider themselves just as powerless and hopeless. These include persons in unfulfilling job situations, those who feel trapped in unhappy marriages, the ones in a financial bind, those whose health is failing, and so on.

They all have one thing in common: They are certain they are powerless to change the situation or condition and they may become either extremely passive or overly aggressive. Their belief in their inability to improve their situations is essentially false. Unfortunately, as I have written many times, it is true if they believe it to be true.

It is tragic that so many have fallen into a state of despondency because of the false belief in their limitations.

When one is in this state, his thoughts become habitually negative. Even though many aspects of his life are positive, his attention will always be focused on his failures and shortcomings. This reaction is often caused by the attitudes of those who have authority over their lives. Teachers or parents, for example, learn to expect certain behavior patterns from youngsters. If a student is labeled "bad" in a teacher's mind, almost any type of behavior will be judged from within the framework of that opinion. The same behavior from the student labeled "good" would pass unnoticed.

The "bad" child is constantly being condemned, even when this judgment is not warranted and the "good" child may receive undeserved praise. Thus, "the bad get badder and the good get gooder."

As a result, the "bad" person becomes resigned that this is the way he is and never makes the effort to change or to try to better the conditions in which he finds himself. If he becomes overly aggressive, it is because it is his way of attracting attention.

Many of our problems stem from the false assumptions we are constantly making, especially about ourselves.

We may be weak in a certain area and mistakenly accept this weakness as being irrevocable. Instead of endeavoring to overcome it, we give it the power to make us feel inferior or guilty.

We assume that people are scorning us because of this weakness and become filled with self-contempt. We don't like ourselves and so assume that others don't like us. Before long, we find ourselves becoming hostile, critical, and filled with hate. Almost all overaggressiveness and violence stem from weakness.

Don, formerly one of the toughest of convicts at Folsom Prison and now a prominent graphologist and reflexologist, found the answer, as he revealed to me in a letter. He wrote:

"I understand hate very well. I lived it so long that it was a part of my every action, and I wasn't even aware of it. I can now see it in other people, just as you saw it in me years ago in those cold walls of Folsom Prison.

"My hate put me in prison, so I guess my lack of hate is keeping me out. Strange how people look all their life for something to make them happy when all they have to do is rid themselves of their negative emotions and they find that happiness was there all the time."

21

Failing Takes Effort Too

"What might have been" are the saddest of all words.

What a tragedy it is, when our days are ended, to discover that we had the talent and ability to accomplish much more than we did. It will be true, however, for many.

Do you ever experience a vague feeling of discontent because you know you are not living up to your potential? Deep down inside, we all know we could do better. Therefore we should do better. People say success is not worth the effort, but they forget it also takes an effort to fail.

"Success is not worth the price you have to pay for it," they say. But isn't there a price for failing? We like to think that what we do with our lives is an individual matter and the decisions should be ours alone to make.

The parable of the talents in the Bible belies this notion, however. In this story, a master had three servants. Before leaving on a long journey, he gave one ten talents; another, five, and the third, one talent. Upon his return, he found that the first two had put their talents to work and had doubled them. Their master praised them. The third, however, had buried his one talent in the ground, so he still had only one.

The master called him not only lazy, but also wicked. He took the talent from him and gave it to the one who had twenty. Perhaps the lesson to be learned is that we are morally committed to use the abilities we have been given.

There are deterrents to our using our talents and abilities and reaching our potential. We permit what has gone before to be a factor and judge what may be possible by what we and others have done in the past.

This approach may cause an imaginary screen, called the screen of logic, to be placed between our conscious (intellectual) mind and our subconscious (creative) mind. A desire to accomplish something is born, but before we start, we begin to doubt that we will succeed.

Success does not seem logical, either because we or others have failed in the past or because it is a new undertaking. Our desire to achieve is never fulfilled, because it did not pass through the screen into the subconscious, which would have found ways to ensure its fulfillment.

That imaginary screen prevents us from attempting many things we might have accomplished if we had tried. The body and mind work in conjunction with each other in strange ways. It is the conscious, thinking mind that decides what the body is capable of accomplishing. If that part of the mind could be bypassed, apparently there would be no limits to what we could do.

This observation is proved by the unbelievable feats of strength accomplished by people under extreme stress or danger, such as those who have lifted a car and extricated a loved one.

Here is an example of the part the mind plays in determining the extent of one's accomplishments. Ten of the world's greatest runners met not long ago for a mile race in England. The man who finished first, Sebastian Coe, set a new world's record of 3:48.9. The one who finished last was timed at a shade over 3.55. Yet until 1956, it was considered physically impossible to run a mile in four minutes!

What happened to cause this improvement of performance in so short a time? Once the four-minute barrier was broken by Roger Bannister, it no longer appeared insurmountable.

The screen of logic had been removed from the minds of all runners. They had to believe it was possible now because it had been done, and the four-minute mile became almost commonplace.

Many people are depressed and bored with life. They feel sorry for themselves, hoping something will happen to relieve them of their depression and boredom. When they reach this state, they are probably contributing very little, and their abilities are not being used. As life has a way of giving us back what we give out, the situation grows progressively worse.

As in the parable of the talents, even the little that one has is taken from him. This result is neither fair nor unfair. It is simply a law of life.

There is a wonderful prescription. It is much more effective than any pill, sermon, or philosophy. It is to act and to use the talents that have been committed to you to use.

22

Communicating With Your Children

Parents ask me for advice on communicating with their children. Here is the best advice I can give:

When young, consider that you may one day be old; and when you become old, remember that you were once young.

This isn't as easy as it sounds. We go through many changes in a lifetime. The world appears in an entirely different light to a boy or girl of 15 than it does to an adult of 40. This disparity could be overcome more easily if the person who is 40 would make the effort to remember how things appeared to him at 15. The youth has no conception of how the world appears to an older person — and won't have for many years to come.

It seems to me that being young today must be more stressful than it was in the past. I base this observation on the fact that youths have many more choices and decisions to make than did those of my generation. We had plenty of opportunities to get into trouble, but there was one big difference which made it simpler for us. The consequences were much more definite then.

71

If we did wrong, we knew we would have to face those consequences. If we cut school very often, for example, we would be suspended. We and our parents would be disgraced. Knowing that certain punishment would follow any wrong-doing made it easy to decide to behave.

Many parents make life difficult for their children unknowingly. By not laying down definite rules and limits, they leave their children with the necessity of deciding what they should do or not do. They may not be mature enough to do this, so their decision is frequently the wrong one.

This is the reason many young persons feel unloved.

The well-meaning but ill-advised parents do not realize this. They believe they will gain the love of their children by removing restrictions and granting more and more privileges, but this is seldom the case.

We should all have to earn the right to make decisions, and this right should come to us gradually as we prove we have gained enough maturity to do so.

Any other way is unfair to youth. It is similar to tossing someone into deep water before he has learned to swim. It is more sensible to start with the wading pool.

All these factors result in a breakdown of communication between child and parent. Each becomes resentful of the other because of the lack of understanding.

Try this: When your children are speaking, listen to them from their viewpoint, not yours. So often we put our own interpretation on what others are saying, instead of allowing them to express their own ideas. Let them know you are interested in their true feelings, even though you may not always agree with them. This approach alone should improve communication between you.

Ask yourself this question: If you were a youth today under the same circumstances your child is now experiencing, would you be acting differently?

Be fair. You must pretend you haven't had the benefit of all the experiences during the intervening years. Also, you would have parents with whom you were having trouble communicating, just as your child has. This perspective may enable you to be more tolerant.

Another factor may be contributing to your communication problem. You may hold prejudices, many of which were handed down to you from your parents, but which are now antiquated. This generation, for example, is not so prone to judge and classify people as you may be.

Being older, and therefore more set in your ways, you may find it difficult to rearrange your thinking and opinions along certain lines.

You can't understand your children's viewpoints because they often differ from yours. Keep in mind, however, that this process works both ways. Your children often cannot understand your viewpoint either.

A quiet, unbiased discussion might prove beneficial. Just make sure it doesn't end in an argument or a shouting match. Now is the time to make every effort to open the communication channels. It becomes increasingly difficult to do so as the years go by. You will be pleasantly surprised to find your children are just as anxious as you to have a close relationship.

Communication means expressing your feelings, and permitting others to express theirs.

23

A Wonderful Example of Courage

An inspiring letter from a stranger has caused me to realize how much some people can accomplish, even though suffering from severe physical disabilities. It came from a reader who gave his name and address but wishes to remain anonymous. He wrote:

"Polio left me paralyzed from the neck down in infancy. Today, at age 31, I have recovered 30 percent use of my left arm and hand and can sit in my wheelchair three hours a day (if someone has the time to lift me into it).

"I became discontented from age 12 to 20 as I became very aware of sports and girls. Although I was adjusted to being a shut-in, I had never accepted permanent paralysis. At age 20 I was four feet, six inches tall, paralyzed, and deformed. Also, I was terribly dependent.

"As you suggested in one of your columns, I had a mental picture of myself of the ideal way I would like to be: A tall, strong athlete dating girls. You wrote further, 'Discontent is the penalty we must pay for not being thankful for what we have.'

"I gradually came to realize this. I was cared for and I could see, hear, feel, and think. I believed it would be better to be dead from the neck up than from the neck down. "You said, 'The way to ensure a richer life and a more fulfilling existence is to increase your contributions to life.' I asked myself, 'How could I, a dependent paralytic, contribute or make contributions?' "

I have found this to be true in hundreds of so-called "hopeless" cases. If a person has a strong desire for something, can conceive of it happening, and plant the seed in his mind, life seems to respond. Events will inevitably take place and point the way to its fruition. This man developed a strong desire to contribute, even though at the time this appeared to be an impossibility. Here is what happened: "A friend who was filled with wisdom came to see me and spoke clearly. He said, 'You will always be a shut-in paralytic. You must make a life for yourself. If you want to contribute, here are names and addresses of other shut-ins. Send them cards and notes.' "

"I did this as a contribution and didn't expect any answers. A few days later, I received letters from many with disabilities. These letters have developed into close friendships. "Then you wrote, Make a mental picture of the ideal you as you would like to be.' In my case, I changed this to 'can be.' You added, 'Try to do a little more than you have to do. Trying can be the difference between success and failure.'

"How true. How could I learn to write with a partly paralyzed left arm and hand, feed myself, stay alone for hours? I did and now I can.

"We all must mature dispite our circumstances. Today, at age 31, I am a bed-fast quadriplegic shut-in, but I have perfect teeth, thick black hair, good hearing, fair vision, a pretty good brain, and a lot of good pen friends.

I enjoy watching birds and seeing beautiful flowers. "Sure, I know what I would like to be, but I can be what I can be. Thanks for everything."

The law of compensation is a great equalizer. It gives people like this young man more actual happiness than "luckier" people will ever experience. Succeeding in his efforts to learn to use his paralyzed arm and hand to write, and then to receive mail in return, probably gave him a higher level of joy than you and I will ever know. We have all seen examples of this situation. The person for whom we feel sorry might well feel sorry for us who appear to be more fortunate. Many persons are bored and frustrated because of a false belief in their own limitations. They hope for changes in their lives, but changes won't come until they themselves change. These negative beliefs must be dropped.

Each of us can play a large part in determining our future. But we must take the first step.

24

Life Ruined by Negative Self-Image

This story illustrates the devastating effects of a negative self-image.

Although only in his early thirties, Mark had already spent several years in prison. His early childhood had been very traumatic. His parents, but especially his grandfather, treated him in a manner that would be inconceivable to most of us. They made him feel he was absolutely unworthy and subjected him to extreme physical abuse.

Nevertheless, Mark had a brilliant mind. I recognized this fact immediately when he became a steady member of my group at Folsom State Prison. I hoped that if he were ever released, he would find a way to live up to his potential. His release did come, and we became fairly good friends. He was granted a scholarship to college and earned straight "A's," even though carrying many units. Mark became a teacher, while still a student himself, and gained a large following and a fine reputation.

Later, he initiated a program to help ex-convicts back into the outside world through education. I was very proud of him and confident that he would make a very valuable contribution to society.

It was not to be, however. Despite his achievements, he apparently was unable to overcome his innate low opinion of himself. It was almost as though Mark set out to destroy everything he had created. He began to drink heavily, and it was only a matter of time before his new world disintegrated.

He is now back in prison.

This was a case of self-destruction, almost done deliberately. Despite his magnificent effort and accomplishments, the negative influences of his childhood were too deeply ingrained in his subconscious for him to overcome.

Mark's story is not at all unusual. A survey was made recently to determine what had happened to the quiz program winners of the sixties who had won $75,000 or more. As well as could be determined, not one now has any more money than he had before his windfall. The same is almost always true of sweepstakes winners and others to whom money comes in an unexpected and sudden manner. Various reasons are given for this situation. Lack of experience in handling money is a logical one, and no doubt this does play a part.

In my opinion, however, there is a much more important factor. This shows up in other areas of one's life, as well as in matters where money is involved. These people had a poor self-image and didn't really believe they deserved their good fortune. If you obtain something you do not think you deserve, it will make you uncomfortable, and you will subconsciously take whatever steps are necessary to relieve yourself of it.

Those with a poor self-image are disturbed by anything that does not reinforce their negative beliefs about themselves. Therefore, as incongruous as it seems, a sudden stroke of good fortune is almost unwelcome. After all, it forces them to admit that they are not as bad off as they like people to believe. Check this observation with people you know. See how many will admit, even to themselves, that they have finally reached the point of financial independence.

What about the one who is married to an alcoholic who has recovered? Is that person, who formerly was so miserable, now happy? Probably not, because the excuse for indulging in self-pity has been taken away from him, and his friends no longer feel sorry for him. As a result, the one married to a reformed gambler or alcoholic is likely to divorce that one and marry another with the same weakness the first spouse had.

Those with a low opinion of themselves have probably been bombarded with negative thoughts ever since early childhood. Nevertheless, they will have to take steps to change this opinion if their life is to be happy and productive.

For some reason, most of us underrate our accomplishments while overemphasizing what we think are our failures. We should keep in mind that to fail in one aspect of life is not to fail in life.

25

In Everything Give Thanks

Over the years, I have gained a different perspective concerning Thanksgiving Day and the true meaning of giving thanks.

This has helped to explain a Bible passage I have often quoted but never was able to understand: "In everything give thanks" (I Thessalonians 5:18).

In our large family, Thanksgiving Day had always been filled with excitement. My mother and father always made it a festive occasion, no matter how strained the financial circumstances at the time. Each year, I would write down all that I felt I should be thankful for. Some years, I must admit, the list was quite small, although I would try my hardest to stretch a point wherever possible.

I continued this practice into adulthood.

One year, for some reason, I decided to list the "things to be thankful for" on one side of the paper and the "things not to be thankful for" on the other.

A few years ago, I came across this list, which I had written so long ago. I was amazed at what I saw.

Events of the intervening years made me want to revise the list almost completely. In many instances, as things turned out, I should have given thanks for that which was listed on the "not thankful for" side, and the opposite was also true. That experience completely changed my thinking and attitude concerning my day-to-day happenings. It has helped me to withhold judgment as to whether what happens to me is "good" or "bad."

There is an ancient Chinese tale about an old man whose manner of looking at life was entirely different from that of others in the village. We could all learn something form his philosophy.

It seems this old man had only one horse, and one day it ran away. His neighbors came and commiserated with him, telling him how sorry they were for the misfortune that had befallen him.

His answer surprised them.

"But how do you know it's bad?" he asked.

A few days later, his horse came back, and with it were two wild horses. Now the old man had three horses. This time, the neighbors congratulated him upon his good fortune.

"But how do you know it's good?" he replied.

The next day, while attempting to break in one of the wild horses, his son fell off and broke his leg.

Once again, the neighbors came, this time to console the old man for the bad luck that had befallen his son.

"But how do you know it's bad?" he questioned.

By this time, the neighbors decided his mind was addled and didn't want to have any more to do with him.

However, the next day a warlord came through the village and took all the able-bodied young men off to war. But not the old man's son, because he was not able-bodied!

We would all lead much more serene lives if we were not so quick to pass judgment on events as they occur. Even that which you resent the most, and which still causes a negative reaction when it comes to mind, may have played a positive part in your life.

Perhaps in looking back, you will see that it was exactly the experience you needed to further your development. It helped to make you the well-rounded person you are now.

Wighout that particular experience, which you have resented for so long, you would not have gained the understanding and compassion you now possess.

Now, because of your increased knowledge and growth, you are ready for whatever wonderful new experiences are in store for you.

Therefore, "In everything give thanks."

More often than not, future events will prove your faith was justified.

26

Act As If Failure is Impossible

Among subjects frequently mentioned by readers is this: "I set goals and decide to start a new project but become discouraged and never begin. If I do, I invariably stop short of completion."

At first I gave this matter little thought and probably responded in a routine manner. As time went by and my contacts grew, however, it suddenly became apparent to me that this was a common problem. I realized that there must be much talent going to waste because it causes one to live a dull, lackluster life when the same person could just as easily live a life full of excitement or, at the very least, one full of interest.

Strangely enough, it takes about as much energy to fail as it does to succeed. It requires energy to resist motion. One has to make a decision to do nothing, the same as one has to make a decision to do something.

The difference is contrary to what one might believe. The person doing nothing is more tired, in the long run, than the active one. The one who does nothing experiences nothing, not even in rest. In fact, the opposite is more often true. Inertia, or lack of accomplishment, actually drags one down.

It causes a sense of dissatisfaction that even drugs or alcohol can erase only temporarily. Inertia doesn't come easily, no matter what you may have been led to believe. The active person, whether materially successful or not, has one thing going for him that the inactive person does not have. He knows he is moving forward toward personal growth. I am convinced there is inherent in many people a will to self-destruction. They think of themselves as losers, so it seems mandatory that they prove their self-appraisal is correct. It is easy to make excuses. We tell ourselves we are not making a sincere effort because "we are not in the job best suited for us" or "our boss would not appreciate it anyway." We find endless reasons for not accomplishing more. The truth is we use as much energy in time-consuming pursuits as we would if this energy were directed to more positive undertakings. It takes character to put forth extra effort, especially if you can't be sure it will pay off in a material way. Therefore, it is easy to get in a rut and never use more than a fraction of your ability.

I sometimes wonder whether a person refrains purposely from making the effort, as difficult as it would be for him to admit it to himself. After all, if he can convince himself he is very busy, even though with inconsequential things, he can rationalize that he doesn't have time to do something constructive.

Even though one may be entirely unhappy with present circumstances, the prospect of change, even though it might be for the better, is abhorrent to some people. Many will attempt to fool themselves and others by trying just hard enough so they can say they did try. This eases their conscience and justifies their giving up.

"I tried but I was too old (or didn't have enough time, education, or money)," they convince themselves. "Now I can sit back and watch others who are better qualified (or luckier) fight the battle."

It is true that some pain can be avoided by not disturbing the status quo. The rewards and satisfaction to be gained, however, more than make up for any discomfort. An undertaking which culminates in success brings a sense of satisfaction. The one who does not make the attempt will never experience this. If a person has a sincere desire to move in a more positive direction, he must change his attitude regarding past failures. The memory of these causes him to back away from making a sincere effort to succeed. One should regard each failure as a learning experience and as a step toward his ultimate success. Therefore, it was not a failure at all!

When this is done, and all mental blocks removed, there is one more procedure to take. One should start with the attitude that success is a foregone conclusion. Although it is to be recognized that obstacles may appear, act as if failure is impossible.

The next time you set a goal for yourself, start with this attitude. You will soon discover that all the limits you imposed upon yourself are false.

27

Methods of Overcoming Habits

Of all the problems that plague people, unwanted habits seem to be near the top of the list. I think I receive more letters on this subject than on any other. Here is a typical one: "All my life I have been haunted by habits, until I have reached the point where I feel they control my life. Perhaps you could explain what a habit is and how I might learn to control them better. Also, any hints you could give me to help me overcome them would be appreciated."

I cannot guarantee that the answers I give to questions asked apply in every case. Sometimes one has to find the answer to his problem within himself. However, I have gained enough confidence through the years of teaching these principles in prisons to know that the principles themselves are infallible. Whether they work for you or me depends upon our putting them into practice. It is these principles upon which my answers are based.

William James, the late American psychologist, said that anything you do 45 times in a row becomes a habit. I don't know how he decided upon the number 45, but it sounds logical.

86

Before we go into the subject of breaking bad habits, however, let us take the positive approach. Few do this in regard to habits. What James said about bad habits must also apply to good habits. Therefore, 45 consecutive days of fulfilling any commitment, such as sustaining an exercise program, not smoking or drinking, jogging, or working toward whatever goal you have set for yourself, should ensure the continuation of a good habit just as it would a bad one.

Eastern teachers explain habits this way: The continuation of a thought or act for any length of time causes a groove, rut, or channel to form in the brain. They say the brain is similar to clay, in which channels are easily formed. Once this happens, a person's thoughts will naturally continue to flow in that direction, because it is the line of least resistance. His actions become subconscious or automatic. It takes an act of the will to refrain from doing that which has become habitual. At first, the opposite was true.

When one starts to smoke, he thinks about lighting up. After a while, he lights up without thinking. When you reach this stage regarding any act, you will know you have the habit. Then the groove or channel can only grow deeper.

At this point, two moves will be necessary if the habit is to be broken. The first is obvious: Try to stop or cut down whatever you wish to stop.

The second step, which is often neglected, is just as necessary if a permanent recovery is to be made. A vacuum is bound to occur, and this vacuum must be filled. It is best if steps are taken in anticipation of this before the habit-breaking attempt is made. If a substitute is not found, the vacuum will be filled by the very habit you have given up.

As you get out of the "rut," and the old channels or grooves level off from lack of use, new ones will be formed, made up of the new interest you have chosen. When this happens — and it will if your resolve doesn't weaken — willpower won't be as necessary as it once was. Your thoughts will naturally flow through the new channels, as the old have gradually faded away.

I have never seen an ex-convict successfully refrain from doing that which originally put him in prison by using willpower. Neither have I seen many heavy drinkers or heavy smokers cut down or stop for any length of time by using willpower.

It is only when one loses the desire to do those things that success is attained. This happens when new interests are formed that are more desirable than the old. Some new undertaking must be decided upon. One's entire attention should be centered on this, and the mind should be directed away from that which is to be discontinued.

The mere thought of giving up a habit can be unbearable. If, however, one's thoughts are directed toward the benefits to be derived from abstinence, and then toward the new interest that has already been developed, eventual success is assured.

As with many facets of life, it is one's inner attitudes which are the determining factor between success and failure.

We first form our habits, and then our habits form us.

28

Feeling Low is not a Crime

Quite often, you will meet people who have apparently achieved all they had set out to do. All their desires have been met, all their dreams realized. They wonder why success has not brought them the happiness they had believed it would when they started out. We all have different goals, but the end result is often the same. The achievement of the goals has not brought happiness.

It is the process of achieving, rather than the achievement, which brings happiness. The achievement itself will remain unchanged, and so may become monotonous. This fact accounts for so many people being unhappy in retirement. Sitting back and resting on their laurels is not rewarding after having devoted their lives to fulfilling work.

They may waste time and dollars trying to find out why they are unhappy. All they need to do is set new goals for themselves and stop thinking of their lives as being finished.

Ralph Waldo Emerson, the 19th Century essayist and poet, explained why a person must continue achieving if he wishes life to be worthwhile: "A man's wisdom is to know that all ends are momentary, that the best end must be superceded by a better."

How many times have you struggled and worked to acquire a particular possession and then, once you had it, scarcely used it?

Even money sometimes falls into this category. Perhaps that is why those with abundance continue to strive for more. I don't believe we should be made to feel abnormal if we are not happy every moment of every day.

Years ago, happiness was considered a blessing, something to be cherished. If one had the "blues," as it was called, it was considered a passing mood, not a symptom of mental illness. The person was not immediately rushed into therapy. More recently, we have been led to believe that feeling "low," even if for only a short time, is a cause for great concern. This can result in severe emotional trauma. Even worse, it might cause one to resort to "happy pills" or alcohol, hoping these will solve the problem. In reality, feeling low was probably only a passing mood or a normal reaction to a traumatic experience. Everyone should have the privilege of feeling "down" occasionally without being made to feel he is ready for the psychiatrist's couch.

It is possible, I am sure, to reach a state of consciousness that would enable one to face any situation in life without reacting in a negative manner.

Perhaps we will all attain this state someday, and it is certainly worth striving for. In the meantime, it seems foolish to attach undue importance to each passing mood. The self-image a person has plays a large part in determining the degree of his happiness and contentment. If you believe in yourself and have a good opinion of yourself, you won't need to be perfect, although you will continue to try to improve.

Therefore, you will be able to cope with brief periods of depression, knowing they are only temporary. On the other hand, if you have a poor self-image, you will constantly overemphasize your faults and shortcomings. If things are not going well, you will blame yourself, instead of accepting occasional setbacks as part of life and then doing what you can to rectify the situation.

Most people are unhappy some of the time. These periods would pass much more easily if the persons would stop worrying about being unhappy. It is not necessary to be anxious and disturbed simply because one is feeling low. This feeling does not require an explanation; it should simply be allowed to pass.

Marriages are being dissolved for no reason other than one or both partners are not as happy as they think they should be. Instead of discovering ways of giving more to the marriage, they blame their partner or marriage itself for their dissatisfaction. They should realize that if they have feelings and emotions, and if they care for someone, it is perfectly normal and acceptable to be affected emotionally — and sometimes adversely — by the other's actions. The more we learn to control our reactions, the less we will be at the mercy of outside circumstances. However, it is not abnormal sometimes to fail in this respect.

Becoming upset for short periods is not a cause for undue concern so long as we don't accept this experience as an unchangeable way of life.

29

Life Changes with a Smile

Life is exciting because it may take very little to change it for the better.

I have often pointed out that there is a very thin dividing line between one who is happy and well-adjusted and successful and one who is not. Unfortunately, many people never cross that line.

In the case I will be discussing, many years passed before the man — whom I'll call Alex — crossed it.

Recently, I saw a notice in a large metropolitan newspaper. It concerned a man who was scheduled to speak to a very influential group of business and professional people. The speaker was Alex, an ex-convict whom I had known for several years because he attended a class I conducted at Folsom State Prison in California. Before I tell his strange story, I want to point out a fact that played an important part in his life. Those in a position to influence us while we are in the formative stage are much more likely to dwell upon our weaknesses than our strengths.

If only those in authority would learn the value of praise! If they would search diligently enough, they would find something positive about us, no matter how insignificant it might be. Were they to do so, we would be encouraged to better ourselves in this, our stronger area. Then we would have confidence to bolster ourselves in our weaker areas.

Alex was about 50 when I met him. He had a completely negative personality. It was obvious he had a very low opinion of himself, and I determined to find some positive aspect which would give him a better self-image. I had learned from experience that, until this happens, no permanent change will take place.

Try as I might, however, I could find nothing positive about Alex. He walked with a slouch, had no friends, seldom changed expression, and never joined in a discussion. The fact that he kept coming to my class made me anxious to help him. However, I didn't want to praise him unless I could be sincere.

One day, unexpectedly, my chance came. I was telling the group how I used to be a sucker for ads that made great promises. I told them I sent in $20 because an ad promised I would be sent something that would make a great change in my life. In retrospect, it was worth it.

I received a large piece of paper, on which appeared the following words in huge letters: "Do the thing you fear to do."

Whether it was worth it or not, the fact that I sent $20 and received nothing but seven words in return sent the men — including Alex — into paroxysms of laughter.

It was the first time I had seen him show any emotion. His whole being seemed to light up. His smile changed his whole personality, and for that fleeting moment, he became a very attractive, dynamic person. It is hard to describe the change.

I sensed this was the opportunity I had been looking for and I asked him to stay after the class.

"Alex," I said, "you don't know this, but when you smiled today you stood out head and shoulders above the rest of the group. You became the person everone would have wanted to call his friend."

Alex got a faraway look in his eyes. "What you say takes me back to my early childhood. When I was in grade school, I laughed a lot and was very popular. Then my father died, and my mother soon married again. My stepfather was a good man, but he was very strict. He considered it a sin to laugh and be joyful, and finally I felt guilty when I was happy.

"It wasn't long before I became very withdrawn and seldom smiled. I guess this guilty feeling has stayed with me ever since. When you told that story today, I couldn't help laughing. It struck me funny. Surprisingly, I felt good for the first time in years."

On my next visit, I could hardly believe my eyes. When Alex came in grinning, he lit up the whole room with his personality. He brought many newfound friends with him. A few months later, he was released, and I never heard much from him again, except for a brief note of optimism for his future.

My reward came when I read the notice of his impending talk. I knew in my own mind that if he had never learned to smile again, this dramatic change in his life could never have happened.

The dividing line between unhappiness and happiness is very thin. You might even be able to cross it with a smile, as did Alex.

30

Look Inward for Strength, Not Outward

Many look to others for peace and security, but it is usually a fruitless search.

As the Buddhists say, "Is your hunger satisfied when another eats?" "Is your thirst quenched when another drinks?"

"By whose efforts will you be enlightened?"

All that is really necessary is that we have confidence and faith in ourselves, and in our ability to handle situations as they confront us. Some may have to change completely their opinion of themselves before this can happen.

Start with the knowledge that much of what happens to you is of your own choosing. This gives one a great sense of power that he may never have recognized. Everyone would like to see an end to his worries, doubts, and fears, but then he proceeds to think and act in a manner that causes these feelings to perpetuate themselves.

We have to understand that we are constantly planting seeds with our thoughts which will eventually objectify themselves. It is one's own inner attitude that is important, not that of someone else.

Don't make the mistake, as so many do, of waiting for something to happen. One's aim should be to make things happen that are of his own choice. This can be accomplished to the extent one is able to control his thoughts. Some people express a desire for more abundance, for example, then proceed to place most of their attention upon lack. Others wish for better health but constantly think and talk about how badly they feel. You must believe that it is possible to change your circumstances, but not until you change inwardly and discard all negative opinions of yourself. Many go through an entire lifetime believing everything happens by chance. "If things break right, I'll land that contract."

This is a foolish way to live. It is denying our God-given powers to help ourselves, and this is contrary to all religions. The Scriptures are constantly reminding us that it is "sinful" not to use our abilities and our talents to better our conditions. They also remind us to look inward for our strength, not outward. Many persons seem to believe there is no purpose to life, so they continue to drift aimlessly. If they have goals, they are to do as little that is productive as possible, and to discover new ways of self-indulgence.

I have no quarrel with them, certainly not from a moral standpoint. I am not qualified to judge, and I am not sure anyone is. However, I feel qualified to make an observation. I have observed many people whose whole purpose in life seemed to be to fulfill their own gratifications with no regard to the consequences and with no respect for others.

I seriously doubt that they are nearly as happy as those who live productive lives. The reasons for this result are obvious. There is a limit to the amount of happiness one can experience through self-indulgence. If you love to eat and drink, for example, you are limited, because you can only eat and drink so much without becoming ill, or at least uncomfortable. Besides, there is a price to pay in the remorse and guilt feelings that follow.

Too much of any pleasurable activity will eventually become boring. This fact may account for the excessive use of alcohol and drugs by those who have no real reason for living. People who have failed to find a purpose for their lives have done themselves a terrible disservice. They have denied themselves much greater pleasure than they experienced through their aimless drifting, even though they may believe the opposite is true.

Inherently, you have as much faith and confidence as anyone, but yours may not be developed. Put it to test by attempting something you dread doing.

To reassure yourself before you start, ask yourself: "What is the very worst that can happen to me if I fail?" If you are truthful, the answer will probably be, "I won't be any worse off than I was before I tried."

The point we so frequently forget is that each person must find his own way. The more time you waste coveting someone else's talents or possessions, the longer it will be before you discover your own.

31

Yesterday Ended Last Night

There is much talk of stress today, and understandably so. There have been so many changes in our daily living in the last century that it is remarkable we have been able to cope and adjust as well as we have. Although stress is not recognized as a disease, it is certainly the cause of many diseases.

There was probably much less stress in olden times. Then, one could respond to a stressful situation by acting in one of two ways: He could face it head-on and fight, or he could run away — the fight or flight response. In either case, the situation was over with, at least until the next danger appeared. Today it is different. We seldom have either of those two alternatives. Some are under a stressful situation must of their lives, especially if they own their own businesses or hold jobs they dislike, or have an unhappy relationship with someone. These people feel trapped and believe there is no escape

This is not true.

It is another of the false beliefs we have blindly accepted. I have seen too many people relieved of stressful conditions to believe it. However, relief won't come until the person learns where to look for it.

The basic premise behind this column has always been that everyone, no matter what his present circumstances, has the power within himself to change them. This can more often be done by changing himself than by looking for a change to take place on the outside. If you react in an agitated manner when something irritates you, it causes physiological changes which gradually undermine your health.

When you face a situation that cannot be avoided, learn to control your reaction to it. Your life may depend upon your ability to adapt to stressful situations. If you can't fight or run, as your ancestors did, you can learn to adapt.

For example, if you drive in heavy traffic every day, realize how important it is to learn to accept it. Many people do no consider that there is an alternative or that they have a choice, so they are constantly in a state of agitation.

Here are some thoughts from previous columns on how to adapt to stressful situations:

Don't give others the power to upset you. It is probably not the way the peron is acting that bothers you as much as the fact that he is not acting in a way you think he should act. Drop your preconceived ideas of what others should or should not do. It is important that you mentally release the person or persons who upset you.

None of us can think more than one thought at a time. Therefore, let your mind dwell on pleasant experiences as much as possible. One's happiness is not dependent upon overcoming problems, no matter what he may think. One's happiness is dependent upon his ability to change his attitude toward his problems. There is a big difference.

Many people have a part of their lives that is unpleasant. They have accepted the fact that, unless that particular situation changes, they are destined to remain unhappy.

They believe that certain conditions must be met before things change for the better. Their subconscious mind accepts this belief, and it becomes fact. Whatever you believe is true, so far as you are concerned.

One should not accept this false premise. Why should your happiness be dependent, or contingent, upon a situation changing?

To relieve yourself of stress, mentally see yourself as being happy in the same circumstances that now are upsetting you. You will never eradicate an unpleasant situation by giving it power to bother you.

If you learn to accept happiness in the present, despite undesirable conditions, those conditions must change to correspond to the change in your attitude.

If something unpleasant happens, accept it if you must, then adjust to it. This will make it easier to take steps to rectify it. Destructive as it may appear, don't give it power to become a negative factor in your life. Many persons make the mistake of giving too much power to the past. This can be a cause of stress too. It is true that what you did yesterday will have an influence on what you do today if you allow it to do so. However, this also means that what you do today will have an influence on what happens to you tomorrow.

The difference is that you can choose the way you will act today, but what you did yesterday is already done.

Yesterday ended last night.

32

Overcome Negative Cycles

One of the many joys of writing a column is receiving letters from readers.

Some make comments, some ask questions, and some tell how they have used the principles to improve their lives. Here is a question asked by a 40-year-old man: "A few years ago, I had an unexpected setback in my personal life. It seemed to trigger a series of setbacks that haven't stopped yet. I almost hate to get up in the morning because I fear what will happen next. How do you account for this and how can I reverse the trend?"

I think that we have all noticed that our lives seem to go in cycles. Everything goes smoothly for a while, and nothing goes wrong. Suddenly the trend changes, and nothing we do is right.

Some attempt to explain this problem scientifically. They say, and I think rightfully so, that one's cycles influence to some extent our ability to cope with our problems. Regardless of the reasons, these cycles do occur and therefore must be dealt with. As is usually the case, if we understand something, its power to upset us is diminished.

Possibly it was a lack of understanding that contributed to the questioner's problem and prevented his negative cycle from changing. He permitted his original setback to put him on the defensive.

This often happens in the case of a divorce or sudden loss of a job. The person suffers a loss of self-esteem and declines to try anything new because of a fear he might "fail" again. Unless a conscious effort is made, he may never emerge from his negative mood. The more time that is allowed to elapse, the more unlikely is a change for the better. His mood of depression causes him to expect the worst and so he attracts the very things he wants the least. With his self-image lowered, there is a danger he will succumb to that most dreaded of maladies — self-pity.

The only remedy I know that is really effective is for one to take his attention away from his problems and concentrate upon those things he would like to experience. Whatever we give our attention to and allow our minds to dwell upon becomes our experience. It is most important that one force himself to become interested in others and to proceed to build up his self-esteem. This can best be done by setting goals, small at first, then making absolutely sure each goal is reached.

I suggested to the man who wrote to me that he begin developing a talent that has been lying dormant. He chose art and has become so proficient that he has already sold some paintings. His negative cycle has become completely reversed. It is most important to realize that some action must be taken. One cannot sit back and hope for a change for the better without taking the first step.

Another person wrote the following:

"My son has been sentenced to prison. I have been conditioned to believe that every convict is some kind of animal and incapable of anything but violent behavior. Have you ever witnessed acts of kindness and compassion?"

I was happy to be able to answer her in the affirmative. Acts of kindness in a prison are commonplace, although you seldom hear of them. Violence gets publicity.

I told her of a black man who had spent years in prison and escaped. He spent many days in an uninhabited area, not many miles from the prison, looking for a chance to reach a far-off city to make a new start. He heard sounds of distress and followed them cautiously until he found their source. It was a prison employee who had been tracking him and who had fallen and was badly injured. He was unable to walk and was resigned to death.

The convict, Frank, fully aware of the consequences, carried the man back to civilization. Many were to marvel that he was able to accomplish this, because of the distance and difficult terrain.

Despite his act of compassion and the saving of a prison employee's life, Frank was returned to prison. He was later released, but between the time of his return and his release, I came to know him. This was the man I have told about who visualized himself as a songwriter and subsequently had many songs published, although he had never written a song in his life

Good can be found in every situation, every place and every person.

33

Self-Discipline Means Freedom

What is the dividing line between enjoyment and compulsion? Why do some become addicted to a thing while others are able to take it or leave it alone?

For example, to many persons, drinking alcoholic beverages, smoking, gambling, and so on are only diversions to be enjoyed occasionally. To others, they become deadly addictions, taking priority over everything in the person's life. This truth was brought to my mind recently. I was in my car, waiting for the traffic signal to change at an intersection. An old man, shabbily dressed, staggered to a trash can nearby. He rummaged around and came up with an almost empty wine bottle. Putting it to his lips, head back, he apparently managed to drain the last drop. Tossing back the empty bottle, he proceeded on, pursuing his relentless search.

It was obvious that nothing in the world mattered to this individual except where to find more wine. The picture of this man stayed with me, and questions came to my mind.

Where would he be now, I wondered, if he had never taken his first drink? When did the occasional joyous "high" he probably experienced as a youth change to a compulsion that had to be fed? Are there thousands of teen-agers at this moment rapidly approaching the point of no return as he did?

Instead of rummaging through garbage cans, what would he be doing now if he had stopped before it was too late? What talents and abilities would forever remain dormant? How many lives have been adversely affected because at one point in their life they lost the will to say no?

As I drove on, I remembered the times I had similar thoughts regarding the convicts in the prisons I visited. Some had wasted as many as 30 years behind bars cut off from society. Why?

Because at some time in their youth they committed their first theft. Probably it seemed inconsequential at the time. Perhaps they siphoned some gasoline or stole a popsicle. Whatever it might have been, it set the pattern for their future. I frequently wondered where these men would be if they had been able to summon enough self-discipline to say no the first time they were tempted

It may well be that, at the time they committed the act, the question of right or wrong never entered their mind. The only consideration for many seems to be whether they can get away with it. Sometimes this attitude is the result of the example set by one's parents or others one should be able to look up to and respect.

Regardless of the reasons or excuses for their being in prison, however, they would not be there if they had not succumbed to their first temptation. A journey in any direction must start with the first step. One can go on with this line of thought indefinitely. The suffering of those with lung cancer would never have had to be endured, in most cases, if they had said no to the first offer of a cigaret — and had continued to say no. The same principle applies to the drug addict and the compulsive gambler.

There is an important facet of life that should constantly be brought to everone's attention, especially to the very young. It is this: If one indulges in a pleasurable activity without restriction or self-discipline, the point will be reached where the activity will no longer be pleasurable. If no restraint is practiced, it will become a need that must be filled, rather than something to enjoy.

There will no longer be a choice of whether or not to do it. The derelict I saw did not just want a drink; he had to have one.

If one continually does what he wants to do, he will no longer be free to do what he would like to do. This has been the effect on many young people. They are losing their freedom at the same time they think they are gaining it.

Rummaging through a trash can, suffering from lung cancer, or losing a home because of gambling seems far removed from the original act. Hopefully these things will happen only to the few. Those few will be those to whom self-discipline is a nasty word, and for them the price they will pay will be high.

Is there a dividing line between enjoyment and addiction? I would think it would be when what one once found pleasurable now becomes a necessity.

34

Think Solution Not Problem

If one's life is full of problems, one factor becomes obvious: That person has accepted the premise that there are no alternatives. He has formed the habit of believing that problems must be a part of his life and does not even attempt to look for the solution.

To begin, one should at least recognize that there might be an alternative. Until one reaches this point, a relatively problem-free life is unlikely, because the person won't try to find the answer. After all, you wouldn't spend time looking for a solution if you did not think one existed.

It is surprising how many simple things in our daily lives that are irritating to us could be eliminated if we made the effort. Instead, we take them for granted, accepting them as a natural way of life.

This fact came to mind recently when I overheard a casual conversation between two men. One was complaining about the terrible traffic conditions he encountered every morning while driving to work. This had been going on for more than two years, he was saying, and was growing steadily worse.

As it turned out, the other man worked in the same district and had once traveled exactly the same route. When the traffic situation became intolerable, however, he began to look for an alternative. He found that be taking a detour he could avoid the bottleneck. Although this added a mile to the trip, it saved one-half hour in time — with much less stress.

The first man had accepted the problem and failed to consider that there might be an alternative. The second man looked for a solution and found it in the form of a different route.

It is too easy to assume an attitude of hopelessness toward a troublesome situation. When this happens, the next step is a feeling of anxiety and self-pity. The will to make the attempt to change the undesired circumstances may be lost forever.

This must not happen. I have seen too many lives wasted because no effort was made to find an alternative to a difficulty. The first step to reverse the situation is to start thinking "solution" rather than concentrating on the problem itself. Write down all the solutions that come to your mind, even though some may seem improbable. Choose the one that seems most practical and then start some form of action.

Next, face the fact that you yourself may be directly responsible for many of your problems, as difficult as this realization is to accept. If you can see that your self-defeating actions are contributing to your troubles, you will be forced to admit that your problems can be over-come by changing your actions. It is simply a matter of refusing to hurt yourself anymore.

This is the only way that you can stop acting in a way that is detrimental to yourself. Only when you realize that the resentments that you are harboring against other people and situations are harmful to you, for example, will you take steps to drop these resentments.

Some problems are very real and can't be changed. What can be changed, however, is your attitude. Try giving the problem another name. Call it a condition, a circumstance, or a challenge. Now, instead of waiting for it to disappear magically from your life because of some outside influence, determine what changes you can bring about yourself. If you cease regarding it as a problem but think of it as a challenge, you may find the problem no longer exists. Many parents find it difficult to bring up children in today's changing world. Once they change their thinking and look upon their task as a worthwhile challenge and responsibility, they may find it much easier to cope.

If problems continue to plague you in your daily living, realize that you are at least partly responsible. Everyone must face some unpleasant experiences. We must recognize there is an answer to every problem and then set about finding it.

35

Negative Emotions are Destructive

If our lives have been a series of unpleasant experiences, there must have been a reason. Something is obviously happening to prevent us from having pleasant experiences.

This explanation is easy to accept. What is sometimes difficult to understand is that we might be the cause of that "something." One cannot think one way and be another. Whatever one is inwardly must eventually express itself in his life. Those who constantly talk and think about their ailments, for example, are almost sure to continue to experience poor health. Those who think "lack" will continue to suffer lack. It could hardly be otherwise. The "something" that is causing unhappiness may be nothing but the negative emotions that have become an integral part of the person's life. Those who indulge themselves in thoughts of greed, envy, hatred, and resentment have no reason to expect anything different in their own lives. They are virtually locking the door on any good they might experience. It is useless to hope for a better life until these negative feelings and attitudes have been discarded.

We see examples all around us of the great part negative emotions can play in a person's life. One that comes to my mind immediately is that of a man named Robert who spent many years of his life in prison.

Robert blamed his parents — his mother in particular — for all his troubles. As the years in prison mounted, so did his resentment toward her. In fact, he gradually came to hate almost eveyone he had known on the outside. For some reason, he held them responsible for his predicament. In short, he blamed everyone but himself. Naturally, all contacts with people had long since stopped, and he resented this fact too. It was difficult to convince him that his misery was mostly of his own creation. When he finally gained enough understanding to admit this might be partly true, he believed it was too late to do anything about it.

Robert's case was so extreme, and his life at such a low ebb, that the other convicts in the class took a personal interest. I suppose they saw a little of Robert in themselves. At any rate, they agreed to "pull" for him and cooperate in an experiment: They would try to visualize him once again in contact with his family.

As Robert began to change inwardly, and as he dropped his hateful feelings toward others, subtle changes took place in his life. Men who had previously avoided him now sought his friendship. It wasn't long before his entire attitude toward the world altered completely, and he became a fairly well-adjusted individual.

There is something strange and wonderful about the mind. It seems — and this isn't just my observation, by any means — to be able to transcend both time and space. When one sends forth thoughts with emotion behind them, they somehow make contact with thoughts of others which are of a similar nature. The results are sometimes amazing.

A strange thing happened to Robert. He told me that he had almost completely overcome his strong desire to hear from his mother or anyone from the outside world, because he had discovered contentment within himself. Having dropped his resentments, he had become detached from the whole situation, and he found his happiness was no longer dependent upon others. One day, after seven years without a letter from anyone, he received three. He brought them to our class on my next visit and read them to the group. One was from his mother, and the others from his sister and a former friend.

I have seen first hand too many incidents of this kind to believe they are only coincidents or that they happen by chance. Robert's case wasn't unusual. It was simply a matter of a person's dropping the resentments he had been holding — attitudes that had prevented him from experiencing all the fullness that life has to offer.

Holding on to hatreds and resentments acts as a tourniquet. It stops the flow of good.

36

Any Situation can be Improved

Many unpleasant situations can be improved simply by changing our habitual way of thinking. This is true even though the situation itself remains the same. When we become depressed and frustrated, our first thought usually is to look for someone to help us out of our depression and frustration. We hope desperately that we will be shown the "how to" method which will bring quick relief or that someone will be able to tell us what missing ingredient must be added to our life to make it more bearable.

The truth is that no one, no matter how skilled, can be of much help unless we are willing to help ourselves. When trying circumstances appear in our life, we will respond to them according to the way we have been conditioned to respond by the beliefs we have held. Unless these deeply ingrained inner beliefs are changed, all the outside help and advice in the world will be of little help.

An example is the person who constantly expects certain behavior from others. He has formed the opinion that someone should take the responsibility for his being happy. When the other person acts in a manner which is contrary to his expectations, frustration and self-pity are the inevitable results.

Many problems in our lives would be eliminated if we could rid our minds of the preconceived ideas of the way others should act in given situations. That this is ridiculous goes without saying. Would you enjoy others constantly expecting you to act according to their specifications?

As I pointed out recently, we must discard the belief that others owe us anything. So long as we believe they do, our happiness is contingent upon our being paid, and we will often be disappointed.

As soon as you discard this belief, your fulfillment no longer depends on anything or anyone outside of yourself. Now you can take steps to becoming the independent, well-rounded person you were meant to be. It must become obvious that no permanent change for the better can take place in one's life before a certain amount of de-programming, or unlearning, takes place.

You probably wouldn't think of piling heaps of clean fill dirt upon garbage and then starting to build upon it. It would be much more logical to remove the garbage first. It is the same with the mind. Get rid of all misconceptions first then start the building process. If you persist in holding negative beliefs concerning yourself and your life, you are condemning yourself to living within the framework of those beliefs.

You may strive diligently to develop new ways of thinking but, in a crisis, you will always revert to your habitual manner of responding. It is these beliefs that must be your major concern. When you succeed in changing them, outside help may not be needed.

Many of our problems would disappear if we would learn to rely on our own inner resources. The older one gets, the more he is likely to become as a child, almost entirely dependent upon others for happiness. Imagine the peace of mind of the person who is sufficient unto himself.

You will usually find that whatever you need to solve your problems can be found within yourself, to the extent you are self-reliant and believe in yourself. This statement is not meant to imply that we do not need help at times.

It is the belief that we are not capable and must constantly call upon others to handle unpleasant situations that constricts our freedom and blocks our progress. We might wait a lifetime for someone to come along and save us from ourselves. The knowledge that one's own attitude can improve a situation is a great morale booster. It gives one an inner confidence that cannot be shaken.

Many spontaneous reactions to adverse circumstances are the result of early conditioning. As children, we automatically turned to others for support when we were upset. This was a natural response, but now we must break the habit of being dependent. We will never reach maturity until we do, no matter what our age.

One's outlook on life plays a major part in his happiness, and this is something that only the person himself can change.

37

There is a Way Out

We will answer two questions from readers.

Question: People around me seem to get what they want, or at least most of what they want, but I never do. Have you any idea what I might be doing wrong? I try, but nothing happens.

Answer: You may not be getting what you want, but you are probably getting what you believe you are qualified to have. The chances are great that you do not really believe you deserve the things you want, so you unconsciously hold back from making a determined effort to obtain them.

Before you can effect a change for the better in your outer life and circumstances, you will have to change your opinions and beliefs about yourself. Don't feel guilty if you presently have a low opinion of yourself. We live in such a negative society it is difficult to react in a positive manner.

We are constantly being bombarded with suggestions that we will become ill, slow down as we grow older, or become victims of inflation and a recession. Unless you make a conscious effort to disregard all this negativity, it becomes part of your consciousness, perhaps without your realizing it. Therefore, you will attract those conditions to you. There is nothing mysterious or mystical about it. It is simply a fact that whatever we devote most of our attention to, we will experience. It would be strange if it were otherwise.

Try memorizing the following lines and repeat them constantly until they make a deep impression on your subconscious mind. If you do this, you will see positive changes take place in your life. "I realize that I have the right to choose my own thoughts. I am not bound by anyone else's opinion of me. No one does my thinking for me unless I let them. I am choosing for myself thoughts of health, happiness, prosperity, love, and understanding. Fear, hate, and poverty have no place in my thinking. From this moment on, I am taking dominion of my life."

(The person who asked this question wrote back and said she experienced a tremendous change in her life in less than a week!)

Question: I am bored and have little interest in anything anymore. I seem to have always a vague feeling of dissatisfaction and a sense of hopelessness. Is there a way out for me?

Answer: There certainly is a way out. First, analyze why you feel this way. It is undoubtedly because, deep down inside, you know your life is not what it could be or should be. Naturally, you are bored if you are living far below your potential.

Unfortunately, when one permits himself to reach this state, it becomes a vicious circle. Having lost interest in life, he allows his health to deteriorate. A depressed, unhappy person pays little or no attention to nutrition, a factor which accentuates his depression and thus makes matters worse.

117

When one's health is poor, because of improper diet and lack of exercise, it is very difficult to have a positive outlook. Therefore, I advise concentrating on improving your health first, almost to the extent of making a hobby of it. After that is accomplished, decide on one attribute or talent you possess and determine to develope it.

It wasn't long before the person who asked this question had a new lease on life. He bought books on nutrition and joined a health spa; his health improved greatly.

He then remembered that when he was a high school student, he enjoyed his public-speaking class, even though he was not particularly proficient. He decided to join a local Toastmasters Club and not only made many friends but also became a fine speaker.

He is now in an entirely different line of work with a much higher income. His boredom and depression are part of the past and will never return, because his entire outlook on life has changed.

Many people believe there is a huge gap between what they are and what they would like to become. This is not true. The only requisite is that you must begin to move toward your goal.

38

Adjusting to Each Other

If everyone held the same opinions and beliefs, we would all react in the same manner to every situation. Obviously, this is not the case, and yet we sometimes act as if we expect it to be.

We find it difficult to understand others' actions in certain circumstances if they are unlike what ours would have been. They might act in a way that seems entirely foreign to us, and unless we understand that their conclusions are the result of a different set of beliefs than ours, it could result in serious misunderstandings.

This is what happens frequently in close relationships, such as in a marriage. Two people who come together may have had entirely different upbringings. Their lives were spent apart until they met, so it is only natural that their attitudes concerning many aspects of life may be totally dissimilar.

One's prevailing attitude toward any situation is the result of beliefs and opinions formed in the past. Unfortunately, many of these differences won't be apparent until the couple is living together.

On the surface, some of them will seem inconsequential, but when they continue to appear they can assume great importance. It is especially difficult because something that is of great significance to one may have little meaning to the other.

This is what happens in instances such as one enjoying breakfast while the other views it as a waste of time, or of one being very punctual and the other having no conception of time. These differences require that adjustments be made on both sides. If their overall outlook on life is not the same, serious problems may develop.

The ideal solution is to marry one whose habitual attitude toward life is basically the same as is yours. We often make the mistake of believing we can "change" the other person. The fact must be faced that no one can change another until and unless that individual has a deep desire for the change to take place. At most, you can only be a helpful influence.

If one has been brought up in an environment of negativity, for example, his patterns of thought may be so deeply ingrained that no amount of good fortune could alter his viewpoint. If he marries a person whose outlook is one of optimism, it will not be easy for them to adjust to each other.

In the past, there were fewer divorces because people were more prone to accept whatever life offered without question. They didn't think that it was within one's power to change his circumstances. This premise also applied to one's personality. "I am as the Lord made me, and nothing can be done about it." These, of course, were false beliefs, and people no longer accept them without question. However, if one partner decides to alter his outlook on life, and the other does not, it may cause difficulties in the relationship. Today, marriage partners no longer accept the fact that they must assume a set roie, and so more understanding is required from both than was needed in the past.

There are more options open to the woman of today, and this fact can be a cause of anxiety and mental stress for both partners if the woman is married Even the wife who chooses not to alter her role as a wife and mother is required to make that decision.

It would be much easier in a marriage or any other close relationship if both partners developed and grew at the same pace. But this is seldom the case.With growth comes a completely different outlook on life, and what was once important no longer has any significance. When growth takes place in one and not the other, and conflicts follow, the blame is frequently placed upon the person who has not changed. That may not be fair. After all, that one is still the person you married, whereas the one who is changed is no longer the one the other partner married.

Our reactions to events as they occur in our lives are determined by our past thoughts and beliefs. It follows that future events will be influenced by the way we think today. If our thoughts are negative concerning our marriage, job home, or even our health, we know what we can expect in the future.

39

Utilize Freedom of Choice

There is no situation which cannot be improved. It may be that the situation itself will not change immediately, but it can be made much more tolerable by a change in one's attitude toward it.

This change of attitude will cause one of two things to happen. The situation will either change for the better or a change will no longer be desired.

It was very difficult, especially when I first began bringing these teachings to men in prison, to convince them they could change their lives for the better. However, it soon became evident to many of them that this was possible. Almost as if by a miracle, as they changed their attitudes toward the guards and others in authority, they experienced an immediate improvement.

Surprisingly, many in the outside world also believe they are "boxed in" to hopeless situations. So long as this belief persists, it is very unlikely that a change will occur for the better.

One of the greatest gifts we have been given is seldom used. It is the freedom to determine how we will react to any situation, as well as the freedom to choose what our attitude will be concerning it. If we fail to utilize this freedom of choice, the situation will remain unchanged. The following story illustrates how an intolerable situation can be changed solely by a change in attitude. Hopefully, it will convince us that nothing is impossible if the desire is great enough.

It concerns a young bride who followed her husband to an army camp in the California desert during the Second World War. Because living conditions in that area were very poor, he advised her against the move, but she insisted on being with him.

It wasn't long before she wished she had followed his advice. The heat was terrible, the wind blew constantly, and the sand and dust were everywhere. She grew terribly bored, as the only neighbors were Indians, who spoke little English. As a final blow, her husband was ordered farther into the desert for two weeks of maneuvers. This was too much for Mary, and she wrote her mother she was coming home. Her mother wrote back, and the letter included these two lines:

"Two men looked out from prison bars. One saw mud; the other saw stars."

So Mary determined to look for the stars. She made friends with the Indians and learned enough of their language so that she could converse with them. She asked them to teach her weaving and pottery and became interested in their culture and history. She then decided to make a project of studying and learning about the desert. As her mother sent her books about the various plants and trees, they became things of beauty to her. She eventually became such an authority on the entire area that she wrote a book about it.

It is obvious that outwardly everything in Mary's environment had remained the same. Certainly the desert itself did not change, nor did the Indians. Only the fact that she decided to look for the stars in the situation instead of allowing herself to remain mentally mired in the mud changed an almost unbearable situation into one that was both pleasurable and rewarding.

It is too easy to judge by outward appearances only. This causes us to react in negative ways to situations in our lives without considering that there might be a positive side.

When one mentally accepts conditions as they appear on the surface, he will give up trying to improve them. His world grows steadily smaller, and his capacity to give of himself diminishes. One cannot expect a situation to improve if he believes an improvement must depend upon a change in outside conditions. One must be receptive to the idea that a change in his own attitude may be all that is necessary

40

Desire to Change Life Must Be Strong

It has been said that the only difference between being in a rut and being in the grave is a matter of depth.

Many people are satisfied with life as it is. Although they desire changes that would make it more fulfilling, their desire is not strong enough in any one direction. Because their forces are scattered, nothing of consequence is accomplished.

Believing that a change for the better is beyond their reach, many don't make the effort. This is not true, however. The foundation is already there. It is simply a matter of building upon it. This is so whether that which is desired is an improvement in circumstances or the development of character traits, such as more self-confidence.

Try looking at yourself and your life objectively. Before you do anything, you must have at least some desire to do it. This includes a simple act such as getting out of a chair and walking across the room. With no desire, one would merely vegetate. To accomplish more than you are at present, it is necessary to increase your desire to do more

This is the stumbling block for many people. Their wants are too vague, so all they become are wishful thinkers. There was probably a time in your life when you wanted something so much that you made a great effort to get it. If you were frequently frustrated, you unconsciously made the decision to stop trying.

You may have a desire for something, but the memory of the hurts and disappointments in the past prevents you from making the effort. This causes a feeling of hopelessness, and the rut grows deeper.

Fortunately, there is a remedy, but it takes practice and determination. Choose one desire you would like to see fulfilled above all others and focus your entire attention upon it. Drop some of the vague longings you are holding on to and concentrate on attaining the one. When your mind wanders from one minor yearning to another, bring it back to your main goal. The next step is visualization, and this presents a major, although unnecessary problem for many. Some say they cannot build a mental picture, and so they believe this effective method of goal achieving is denied them. Actually, to make a mental picture of an object, you only need to know what it looks like. You do not have to see the picture in your mind

For example, if you can make a sketch of an elephant without seeing one, you have practiced visualization. Once this block is removed you are ready for the next step. Define your object clearly, making sure it is good for all concerned. Don't share what you are doing with others, for they might talk you out of it. At this point, your self-confidence may not be developed enough to overcome the negative influence they try to impose upon you.

Next, visualize what you want and act as if it is already yours, not that it will be at some future date. It is important that you see the end result and not, at this point, be concerned about the methods to be used.

If your desire is strong — and it will be if you have been persistent in this — you will be led to take whatever steps are necessary for its attainment. Take all of your attention away from the things you don't want and place it upon that which you desire the most. You must be willing, to a certain extent, to give up your present identity and assume the characteristics of the person you aspire to be. Give up all ideas of your present limitations.

Then, even before your goal is achieved, get in the habit of giving thanks. Having the confidence to give thanks for something not yet received is supreme faith.

This may all seem irrational, but it works. It is not necessary that we know how. The process is similar to a seed, which has within itself all that is needed for its self-expression. Once the seed is planted in the soil — in this case, your mind — you can confidently await its expression and be prepared to do what you are guided to do.

41

Discard the Worry Habit

There are methods that can be used to help one overcome the worry habit. Most of us, for example, could face the trials and tribulations of one day. Unfortunately, however, we face the day with the added burdens of regrets about the past and fear of the future.

Thomas Carlyle, the writer and philosopher, had the right idea when he said, "Our main business is not to see what lies dimly at a distance but to do what lies clearly at hand."

Making the choice to look at things differently is another indication of the power we have to control the circumstances of our lives. Most of the great thinkers agreed that living one day at a time makes us much more capable of handling life's problems than if we give power to the past and the future.

Writer R.L. Stevenson said, "Anyone can carry his burden, however heavy, until nightfall. Anyone can do his work, however hard, for one day. Anyone can live sweetly, patiently, lovingly, purely, till the sun goes down and that is all that life really means."

The Bible often mentions the value of concentrating on each day. "Give us each day our daily bread . . . This is the day the Lord has made. We will rejoice and be glad in it . . . Sufficient unto the day is the evil thereof."

In his beautiful poem, "Salutation to the Dawn," the Indian poet Kalidasa wrote: "For yesterday is but a dream, and tomorrow is only a vision, but today well-lived makes every yesterday a dream of happiness and every tomorrow a vision of hope. Look well, therefore, to this day."

William James, the American psychologist, and Lin Yu-tang, the Chinese philosopher, lived at different times but they devised the same method for conquering worry. James said, "Be willing to have it so. Acceptance of what has happened is the first step in overcoming the consequences of any misfortune."

In agreement, Lin Yu-tang said, "True peace of mind comes from accepting the worst. After accepting it, try to improve upon it."

Here are steps one can take to help stop worrying:

— Decide what is the worst that could happen if everything you are worrying about were to materialize.

— Spend your time and energy calmly trying to improve upon the worst, which you have already accepted mentally.

— Make sure you have all the necessary facts and analyze them. Don't just choose the facts that are in agreement with your thinking.

— Arrive at a decision and act immediately. Once you have reached a decision, dismiss all anxiety about the outcome. Don't hesitate or be indecisive.

It is now an accepted fact that worry is detrimental to one's health. If a person could somehow rid himself of all fears, worries, feelings of futility, frustration, anxiety and despair, I'm confident his health would take an immediate turn for the better.

More than 2,000 years ago, Plato said, "The greatest mistake physicians make is that they attempt to cure the body without attempting to cure the mind. Yet the body and mind are one and should not be treated separately."

It is important that one takes responsibility for one's current circumstances, but realistically, not with feelings of guilt. There is no reason to expect perfection of oneself, so why worry if we fall short occasionally?

With maturity comes the realization that we are to blame for most — if not all — of our misfortunes. It is a great plus in our lives when the time comes that we can face this fact, because what we caused we can change.

42

Develop Self-Reliance

The well-adjusted person has one quality that others lack. When something displeasing or unpleasant happens, he first accepts it, then has enough self-reliance to devise ways of solving the problem.

This quality is well worth striving for. Without it, one is bound to be confused because he is constantly open to all the different opinions that are offered by others.

Poorly adjusted people fully believe that others are constantly letting them down. They must face the fact that because they have imposed certain expectations upon someone does not mean that person must live up to those expectations. What right have we to prejudge the way another should act?

Those who habitually rely on their friends to help them through every setback gradually lose control of their lives. They are at the mercy not only of circumstances but also the moods of others. It is a sign of immaturity if a person is so dependent that he is not enterprising enough to solve most of the problems that confront him.

Being always dependent and seeking favors from someone is an almost sure way to end a friendship — not only from the other's point of view, but also from your own. When you put yourself in this position, you may find yourself hating the one who is helping because of your dependence on him. The least that will happen will be that you will become fearful he will withdraw his help.

When it becomes difficult to make simple decisions, one drifts into a state of lethargy and no longer chooses his daily activities. This is an insidious situation, because it can happen before one realizes it. The person completely overlooks the fact that there is an alternative to the dull life he is leading. To these people, even the temporary loss of their television set becomes a major tragedy.

One way to overcome a lack of initiative and feelings of inadequacy is this : Realize you have the power of choice in your everyday activities and exercise this power.

Life does not need to be a series of dull events, one following the other. No one is forcing you always to follow the same routine. No one can prevent you from trying something new and different or from meeting new people and making new friends.

I've seen people turn their lives around completely by simply beginning to think for themselves. They start making decisions and discover, to their surprise, that their lives are in their own hands.

Not being totally dependent upon anyone or anything brings unbelievable peace of mind. When you arise in the morning, you know your day does not depend upon someone's acting in a certain manner. Being self-reliant enables you to set your own pace and to "march to the beat of your own drummer."Also, you will be much more loving and compassionate than you were in the past.

In the long run, we will have to learn to stand alone. Our life is our own. No one can live it for us, nor can we live another's. Each of us must be held accountable for his own acts, and each must reap what he has sown.

If each person must work out his own destiny — and this seems logical — it means that no one can do the work of another. Therefore, the best place to look for help is within ourselves. Once courage and self-reliance are developed, one will find all the help that is needed.

Making decisions is the first step. In the long run, a wrong decision you make may turn out to be superior to one another makes for you. No one can tell at the time what the end result will be.

When you make your own decisions, you are standing on your own two feet! That is the best vantage point from which to meet and face life's challenges. Fear is the greatest stumbling block.

43

Don't Miss Turn At Bat

The best lessons are often learned from the greatest disappointments. That's not much consolation at the time, however.

I recently was asked what was the most disappointing day of my life. The answer came readily to mind, and I'm sure it would be so for the other eight boys who shared the experiences of that day with me — especially poor Joe! I hope they were able to benefit from its lesson as I did later.

It happened back in 1932, the year the Olympic games were held in Los Angeles. I was one of the pitchers for a boys' baseball team. We were participating in an elimination tournament under the auspices of the American Legion.

At this stage of the tournament, one loss would eliminate a team. On this memorable day, we needed only one more win to send us to Los Angeles, where the semifinals were to be held with teams from all over the state.

There was a flu epidemic at the time, and several of the boys on my team were unable to play. Nevertheless, we still had nine of our best players availble. We were confident and determined to reach Los Angeles.

Our team was sponsored by the owner of a sporting-goods store, a Mr. Grodin, who also served as our coach. He promised us that if we won this game, he would arrange for us to attend the Olympic games at his expense. Unfortunately, we wanted to win so badly it affected our play. We were all jittery, played poorly, and went into the final inning trailing by seven runs. Suddenly, as we saw our dreams fading, we came to life.

One base hit followed another until we reached the point where we had the tying run on third and the winning run on second with two outs. Joe, our best hitter, was due to bat. The tension was almost unbearable. Unbelievably, Joe was nowhere to be found! We called time and searched the clubhouse and the surrounding area, but no Joe. It wasn't until later we discovered what had happened to him.

He had made the last out in the previous inning and, believing there was no chance he would have another turn at bat, gone home to hide his disappointment. As we had no one to bat in his place because of the flu epidemic, we were forced to forfeit the game.

No one will ever know if Joe would have delivered the winning hit that would have sent us to Los Angeles to continue in the tournament and see the Olympics. Unfortunately, he gave up too soon, so he never had the chance.

I've often thought about that day. Sometimes, it is virtually impossible to convince people that they still have a chance — that while there is life there is hope. That was my biggest challenge during the years I spent working with men in prison. They think the game is over for them when they still might have another time at bat.

Some of them would argue, "But I have a life sentence, without possibility of parole." Yet I have known three with this sentence, and all three are out now and doing well, so far as I know.

Then the prisoner would add, "I can't conceive of anything that could possibly happen to improve or change my situation."

My answer was always the same: "You are looking in the wrong places for this change. You are waiting for something to happen outside of yourself. You change first, and then, according to the natural Law of Attraction, you will attract whatever is necessary to improve your present circumstances."

It is strange how simple it sometimes is to effect a change in one's life. For several prisoners, all it took was a change in their use of words. One said, "Good morning," to a surly guard; another said, "Thank you," and still another said, "Have a nice vacation."

These simple words were the beginning of a whole new life.

One man, in response to my suggestion to change inwardly, wrote songs and had many published. One studied reflexology, and another graphology. One convict changed his thoughts of his wife from hate to love and was later reunited with her.

If you are thinking about quitting, wait awhile. Remember Joe. The game isn't over yet. You may still have another turn at bat.

44

You Must Be Yourself

It seems to me the last thing most of us want to do is be ourselves.

We cause ourselves much unhappiness by trying to fit into a pattern which is unnatural for us. You might admire a pair of shoes so much that you will insist upon wearing them even though they don't fit. If this is the case, why wear them at all?

No matter how much we may admire someone, we are not and cannot be that person. The more we try to fit into another's pattern of behavior, the more confused and mixed up we become. Even worse, we lose confidence in ourselves because invariably we will tend to underrate ourselves and overrate the other person.

The most miserable people are those who wish they were somebody else. This wish causes one to be constantly pretending to be something he is not. It is one of the primary causes of stress. When you live a lie, you never know when you will be found out, even if only by yourself.

If we realized how little of our own resources we actually use, we would concentrate on developing those we have without envying others for theirs.

It is difficult for many to accept the fact that there is a very thin dividing line between success and failure or winning and losing. For example, in a 100-yard dash the one who finished second may be as little as one-tenth of a second slower than the one who finished first. Just a little more effort might have turned a loser into a winner.

Striving to make the most of the talents we have instead of being envious of others is all that is necessary to obtain success for ourselves.

Before selling yourself short and convincing yourself there is no use trying, keep in mind that you are one of a kind. No one who ever lived has exactly the same characteristics you possess. You may consider some of these characteristics to be liabilities, but this is not true.

Phyllis Diller and the late Jimmy Durante never would have enjoyed the degree of success they did if they had been beautiful and handsome. They each would have spent their time bemoaning the fact that they couldn't pass as fashion models. Instead, they turned what appeared to be liabilities into assets.

Ralph Waldo Emerson, the 19th Century American essayist and poet, wrote in his essay, "Self-Reliance":

"There is a time in everyone's education when he arrives at the conviction that envy is ignorance; that imitation is suicide; that he must take himself for better, for worse, as his portion; that though the wide universe is full of good, no kernel of nourishment can come to him but through his toil bestowed on that plot of ground which is given him to till. The power which resides in him is new in nature; and none but he knows what that is which he can do, nor does he know until he has tried."

It you often envy others their talents, you are probably selling yourself short. Consider these words by the renowned late American psychologist William James:

"Compared to what we ought to be, we are only half awake. We are making use of only a small part of our physical and mental resources. The human individual lives far within his limits. He possesses powers of various sorts which he habitually fails to use."

Why, then, should we wish to be like other people? Some persons feel inferior because there are areas in life in which they don't excel. There is no need for anyone to feel this way.

I know, for example, that a handyman can repair something much quicker and better than I can. Hiring one to do these things for me not only enables him to make a living, but it also gives me more time to develop those capabilities and talents which come more naturally to me. If I felt otherwise, how could I expect anyone to pay me for what I do best?

Peace of mind comes from being and doing what comes naturally to you.

Your success isn't measured by what others can do, but by how close you come to fulfilling your own potential.

45

Victim of the Past

I have written of the trauma which is caused when a person is constantly trying to be someone other than himself. This does not mean one should be as he was when a child, or that he should allow himself to be unduly influenced by the events that took place at that time.

This can be a self-defeating practice. From letters I receive and comments from people to whom I have talked, I have found that many are permitting past experiences to have a profound effect upon their lives. Almost without exception, this effect is of a negative nature.

When not understood, childhood experiences may cause one to act in strange ways without the person being aware of the reasons for his actions. One example is the person who is often on the verge of success in some undertaking. At the point when success appears to be a certainty, however, he somehow finds a way to back away from it.

I didn't understand the reasons behind this situation until a few years ago. I was pleased with the progress a former hardcore convict was making on the outside. I congratulated him by saying:

"Your parents must be very proud to know how well you are doing after such a poor start in life."

This was a mistake. "They must never know about it"' he replied. "They don't deserve the enjoyment my success would give them."

Later, I was to learn that he had turned to a life of crime to "get even" with his parents. He hated them for neglecting him when he was very young. They left him alone night after night while they went on drinking sprees. He was paralyzed with the fear of being alone and would lie in bed trembling for hours, vowing that someday he would make them pay. Whether consciously or not, he chose to commit criminal acts as revenge. After discussing this with me, he understood why he continually refused to accept any good that might come to him. Unfortunately, this knowledge was not enough. Just when he was about to receive recognition for an outstanding job he had done, he committed a "stupid" crime and was returned to prison. I can't help but think he entered the gates with a feeling of satisfaction because once again he had "got even" with his parents.

I have known people who can accept only a certain amount of happiness before they begin to feel guilty. Then, almost as if on purpose, they find a way to destroy their happiness. This is sad, not only because of what they are doing to themselves, but also for what they do to those close to them. It might be well to examine to what extent your life is controlled and influenced by the beliefs you formed when a child. Although you may not be aware of it, your actions are probably confirming those beliefs. If your parents' marriage was a failure, you may have formed the opinion, perhaps unconsciously, that marriage does not lead to happiness. Therefore, even though yours may be successful, you will act in a way to prove your earlier opinion was correct. Then you say, "You see, I was right."

This insight applies to many phases of life. We hold on to our early beliefs, even though they work out to our detriment. Those who have been taught when young that there is virtue in poverty will find it difficult to accept wealth.

If and when wealth comes to them, it won't be lasting. They can't accept it, because it does not conform to their early beliefs. What it amounts to is that we are allowing a child — the child that we were — to direct our lives. The person who has been conditioned to think of himself as a "loser" will invariably find himself on the short end. Even though he finds success, it will be short-lived. His actions will eventually conform to his earlier beliefs about himself. The remedy is not to shut yourself off from the experiences of your childhood. It lies in regarding them as something entirely separate from your present life, except for the messages they have for you.

You cannot change your past, but you can change your attitude toward your past. You have grown and learned because of what you went through. Whatever your experiences, they can be a source of great benefit to you.

46

Be Aware of Power of Words

Words are an expression of thoughts and thoughts create. Therefore, the words one uses regularly and consistently will have a direct effect on one's life.

Teachings such as this were given many centuries ago. For some reason, perhaps because life became more complicated and people grew more materialistic, many simple concepts were overlooked or disregarded. As is true with most life-changing principles, the success achieved is almost entirely dependent upon the extent of one's belief in the principle. Many of the things you are experiencing are, to some degree, reproductions of your habitual thoughts and words. Experiment with different words in order to prove this to yourself. Try the word "sad." Keep repeating it to yourself, and the feeling of sadness will follow, even though there is no outward cause. Now use the word "tired." If you repeat the word often enough, it will naturally follow that you will become tired.

The use of words is particularly effective in determining the state of one's health. Constantly reminding yourself and others of your ill health accentuates the problem. We all need to place more emphasis on the

143

positive aspects of life It isn't necessary that you feel positive in order to act and speak positively. For example, if you wait until you feel well before you think and talk good health, you may never get around to it! Keep in mind that if talking about being tired makes you tired, talking about good health can contribute to making you well.

Faith is the prime requisite to success. The degree of one's faith in anything, either positive or negative, causes it to take physical form. It is next to impossible to talk and think one way and experience the opposite.

To a great extent, we are conditioned to speak in a prescribed manner when we're young. We speak and act in the way we are expected to do. The thought may never occur to us that there are alternative ways. Labels are placed upon us, and we proceed to live up — or down — to those labels.

From time to time, we may have a vague desire to take a step toward our own self-improvement in some area. At this point, words — either our own or those of others — become an important factor. "You're too old." "You don't have enough experience." "It's too late to begin now." "You don't have the right personality." With words such as these, all good intentions go down the drain, and we continue to live in the invisible circle in which we have confined ourselves.

I meet many people who are lonely and unhappy. They wait and wait for something to happen to overcome these conditions, but they are destined to wait in vain. If they could only accept the fact that the power to change these conditions lies within themselves!

The first step one should take is to examine his vocabulary. All negative words relating to himself and his environment must be eliminated. Particular attention

144

should be given to the words used after "I am," because one attracts to himself that which he affirms.

When one speaks positively, he will no longer indulge in self-pity, and people will enjoy his company once again. When friends and relatives call, they will enjoy the conversation.

Now conditions must change to correspond to the way he is speaking, and he has created a whole new world for himself. And it all happened from within.

47

The Most Important First Step

"My greatest want in life is someone who shall make me do what I can," said Ralph Waldo Emerson, the 19th Century poet and essayist.

I agree whole-heartedly. At one time, I believed that the most essential step to a better life was a change in one's attitude toward others and life in general. Now I know there is another step that is even more important: One must first change one's attitude toward oneself!

Unless this is done, the second step is virtually impossible, and many will continue to suffer as they seek in vain for inner contentment.

"Know thyself" is wonderful advice, but seldom followed. I have met many unhappy and frustrated people. Without exception, they have had an extremely limited belief in their abilities.

They live within the framework of that belief and will continue to do so until this belief is changed. They think they have but a small contribution to make to life and so put forth little effort.

It isn't that these people are lazy or lack ambition. I think it is more a lack of knowledge of their potential.

They look for magic formulas that some new "messiah" may have unearthed. They never dream that a new world is awaiting them if they would utilize the resources they already have.

I believe the greatest assistance one can give another is to help a person change his thinking about himself. It is tragic that so much human potential is being wasted.

The most difficult facet of my visits to prisons over the years was to witness so many men leading meaningless lives.

I also was privileged to see the dramatic results of a man's having taken that important first step. This never happened until his opinion of himself was changed. Many wonder how this change can be accomplished. If one has a past record of failures, how is it possible to have a positive self-image?

The mere recognition that the failures were the result of a poor self-image is a good start. Now he knows that his opinion of himself must be changed before an improvement can take place.

The setbacks we have experienced have made an indelible impression on our subconscious mind. This results in our reluctance to attempt something that might result in another failure.

The remedy, and it is infallible if you accept it, lies in adopting the attitude that your success in any undertaking is a foregone conclusion. It is the positive state of mind that one must strive to achieve.

This can be experienced by reflecting on an early success you enjoyed and remembering your feelings at the time. Feel that way now as you move toward your goal. Act as if your success is assured. It seems as though some people fail deliberately. This is not as far-fetched as it sounds. Failing has its rewards. You can tell yourself you tried and therefore have a valid excuse for not trying again.

You can rationalize by affirming that you don't have what it takes or that you are a victim of bad luck. Now you can wallow in self-pity and watch the rest of the world pass you by. Now let's turn this around' because the rewards of success are far greater than the rewards of failure.

In setting your goals, choose those you would select if you believed failure were impossible.

This will require the use of your imagination, which you have allowed to become stagnant. In the past, you half-heartedly set a goal, then deliberately found ways to discourage its fulfillment.

Now you are doing exactly the opposite. You are acting as if the end result is already assured. The confidence and energy this state of mind will generate will insure your success.

This is only one more indication of the power of the mind to control and determine the circumstances of one's life.

48

The Need to be Respected

Sometimes all it takes to change a person's life for the better is to make him feel needed. Perhaps the greatest cause of depression and unhappiness is the feeling one has nothing to contribute.

The following two incidents took place half a century apart, but the end result was the same for both persons involved.

Miss Painter, my fifth-grade teacher, was very strict and could control most of us in the class of 40, but she had no control over Billy.

Billy was everything that was unlikable in a boy. He was sullen and morose and was always getting himself and others into trouble. Because of his negative disposition, he was left out of all activities. At recess, he was ignored and excluded from our games. This situation, of course, only served to make his disposition more intolerable.

At this point, fate stepped in, and the boy's life made an abrupt about-face. Miss Painter became ill, and a substitute teacher was rushed in. There was no time to brief her on the students and their behavior patterns.

Had there been, it is unlikely the subsequent events would have taken place.

The first move the new teacher made was to choose Billy to be the monitor for the week. This choice amused us as we anticipated the mess he would make of his duties. Although these responsibilities were simple, such as passing out papers and erasing the blackboard, there was considerable prestige attached to being the monitor. The results were entirely unexpected. A complete personality change came over Billy with his new-found feeling of importance. He took his new responsibilities seriously and became a friendly and outgoing person. Imagine Miss Painter's surprise when she returned to read her replacement's review of what had transpired during the absence. "You are fortunate to have such a wonderful boy as Billy in your class. He must make your work a joy." Miss Painter shared this review with us in utter amazement. I was to know Billy throughout high school. He became one one of the most popular students in school and was elected president of the student body.

Now the scene shifts. It is 50 years later, and I am conducting a class at Folsom State Prison in California for about 40 convicts. One of them was a man whose name also was Billy. His personality was much the same as that of the young Billy I had known so many years before. He too was sullen and morose and very argumentative.

One day he was being more obnoxious than usual, and I knew something had to be done. Suddenly, my mind flashed back half a century to my fifth-grade class. I remembered the dramatic change that had come over young Billy, and I acted immediately.

"Billy," I said, "I need help, and I think you can give it to me. I need someone to keep track of the books I give out each meeting and to give me a list of names of those present. I'd sure appreciate it if you would do those things for me."

The other men were surprised that I would call on this troublemaker to help me, but they weren't half as surprised as was Billy. He stammered his acceptance and was quiet and attentive the rest of the day. When I came again, I found he had done extensive preparation. He became extremely conscientious and underwent a complete personality change, as had the other Billy so many years before. Apparently, all both Billies needed was someone who believed in them and would be willing to trust them with some responsibility. It is difficult for one not to live up to the expectations of others, whether the expectations be high or low.

A person's opinion of himself will often reflect the opinion others have of him. He will then, perhaps unconsciously, do everything possible to prove these opinions are correct.

49

The Law of Correspondence

"You do not sing because you are happy; you are happy because you sing."

There is deep significance to this statement, which was made by the famed psychologist, William James.

To me, it signifies that the way one feels can be determined to a great extent by the way one acts. It is one more indication that we, as individuals, are not powerless to change and improve situations as they constantly come up in our lives.

Some call this the Law of Correspondence, or consistency.

First, decide what changes you wish to take place in your life, or in yourself. Now develop a habitual mental attitude that would correspond to the new circumstances you wish to experience.

Some will experience difficulty with this idea, being unable to form an attitude which is entirely foreign to conditions as they actually exist.

If this seems impractical, examine your present circumstances from an objective viewpoint.

Do they conform, or correspond, to your mental attitude concerning them? What about your finances? Do you feel trapped and believe there is no chance for improvement? If so, your financial condition is only consistent with your prevailing mental attitude.

It should become apparent that before any area of your life can improve, your mental attitude toward it must change first. To some, this will seem like "putting the cart before the horse."

Your beliefs must correspond to a new, improved condition in your life which admittedly has not yet arrived. Therefore, a physical act may be required which will contribute to bringing about the desired changes.

For example, William James suggested that the act of singing while one is unhappy would have an influence on one's becoming happier.

Suppose you have set as your goal an improved financial state. To reinforce the mental pictures you are making of the improved conditions, spend just a little more money for an article than you ordinarily would. It need be only a few pennies more.

Occasionally have a more expensive lunch than usual.

These are positive acts which will prove that you believe that the desired result is assured. Doubt is the great deterrent to the fulfillment of goals.

The importance of a person's positive mental attitude is proved by the following incident.

A man was very unhappy in his job. It was suggested he write down everything he liked about it — this being a positive act. He protested that there was virtually nothing about it he liked.

"Do you get paid regularly?" he was asked.

"Yes, I do," he replied.

"Do you like that?"

"Well, yes, I like that part of it," he answered.

In a short time, he had written down 17 things he liked about his job. A short time later, he was asked how he was getting along.

"It's really strange," he answered, "how the people I work with have changed."

If you are in a rut, it is literally true as well as figuratively true: Years of habitual thinking along negative lines have caused "grooves" or "ruts to form in your brain.

You may have a sincere desire to channel your thoughts along more positive lines but find it extremely difficult, if not impossible. Your thoughts automatically revert to old patterns.

The Law of Correspondence makes it possible to change undesirable conditions and enables one to become the person he would like to be. All it requires is the ability to control one's actions so that they will correspond to the new conditions and goals he has to set for himself.

Don't make the mistake of wondering how these improvements will come about. Have faith that your life must correspond to the attitude you hold toward life. Then be prepared to act in a positive way.

Release the past and refuse to give it power over you. New, exciting experiences do not come from looking backward, but from looking forward and upward.

50

Why 'Senseless' Acts of Vandalism?

More and more, we hear about "senseless" acts of vandalism. It is true these acts appear to be senseless, but I don't believe this is always true. They make sense to those who commit them. It is admittedly difficult for those of us who consider ourselves to be somewhat "rational" to understand this. However, there are many whose thinking and outlook on life are entirely outside of what is generally considered the norm. Acts of violence and destruction can never be condoned under any circumstances. My point is that there would be much less of this kind of behavior if we endeavored to find the reasons behind it.

I have known many men who have committed acts of extreme violence. Almost without exception, these men were underdisciplined when children. The few exceptions were those who were grossly overdisciplined and who rebelled, but these are in the minority.

Their parents, perhaps fearful of "frustrating" them, denied them nothing. If their children hollered loudly enough, they invariably got what they wanted, whether they earned it or not. As they grew older, these young people faced a rude awakening. They found that life did not respond to their every whim.

It is a tragedy how little regard some parents have for the future of their children, even though I am sure that they mean well at the time. Many of the violent men I have seen in prison have told me they seldom — if ever — heard the word "no" as they were growing up. When they discovered life wasn't that agreeable, they couldn't cope and resorted to violence. This isn't condoning or excusing their actions; it is simply stating what actually happened.

Others with undisciplined childhoods took a different route. Not having developed the inner strength necessary to face setbacks, they withdrew and resorted to drugs or alcohol.

Few of us have escaped feeling utter futility and frustration at some point. You find yourself in a situation and suddenly feel absolutely helpless. Your first impulse is to pick up something and throw it. You refrain, however, only because you have learned a certain amount of self-control.

Suppose you had never been taught discipline and responsibility as a child? Perhaps you would have been one of those who commit senseless acts of destruction.

There can be no question that our early training, or lack of it, must reflect to some degree upon our present actions. All that we are at this moment is the accumulation of what we have thought and done in the past. Unless we take positive steps to change, our future will continue to reflect our past.

Your earlier experiences may have been entirely different from those of your neighbors, and yet on the surface little dissimilarity is apparent. Suddenly one of them commits an act that is abhorrent to you. Who is to say that you, if given the same early environment and conditions, might not have committed the same act?

Many children have never learned the meaning of the words "discipline" and "responsibility." Then, when they reach the stage in life when they must make decisions but discover that life does not hand them what they want for the asking, they rebel.

To strike out in anger and frustration is the only reaction they know. After all, it has brought them what they wanted until now. This is tragic. The child brought up in this manner has no sense of his worth. There has been no opportunity to develop a positive self-image.

If everything he wanted was granted him with no effort on his part, the child never knew the gratification that accompanies earning what one desires. If he has never been prepared for the realities of life, permissive parents and teachers must bear some of the burden of guilt.

The time comes when the young person, consciously or unconsciously, resents those persons who have earned the "good life." When this happens, he seeks to destroy that which he secretly wishes he had worked to acquire. Then we have another "senseless" act of vandalism.